If You Must Work

If You
Must Work

Helps for the
Part-Time Homemaker

Barbara G. Salsbury

BOOKCRAFT, INC.
Salt Lake City, Utah

Library of Congress Catalog Card Number: 76-12309
ISBN 0-88494-300-3

First Printing, 1976

LITHOGRAPHED IN U.S.A. BY
PUBLISHERS PRESS
SALT LAKE CITY, UTAH

Contents

Preface

More and more women are finding it necessary to work. Many contributing factors in today's world are creating these circumstances. Most working women find it difficult to maintain a full-time job and still accomplish the many facets of being a homemaker.

My concern here is not if you choose to work, but if you must. I do not intend to debate whether you should or should not work — if you have a choice. I wholeheartedly support the teachings and wisdom of having a mother in the home.

Since I have been on both sides of the fence, I have been able to see a great need for help, handy hints, ideas, some positive philosophy and encouragement for the women who have to work.

Because you work, your responsibilities are not lessened. No one has said: "If you work, you can relax your efforts around the home fires. We realize you are tired and don't have any time."

When I went back to work I wondered if I was the only one who couldn't seem to cope, was always tired, never had any time, etc. It didn't take me long to discover I was not alone in my heartaches and in my desires to do better. But ·

nowhere could I find any help. I found little information to help me to deal with the situations and problems that confronted me as a working woman and mother. In talking with other women, I found many who were in the same situation.

As research for this book, I conducted a survey of working women to learn where the greatest problems lie. From the survey, I have compiled some suggestions and solutions along with some of my own experiences.

This book is intended to encourage those of you who must work. It presents ideas and thoughts to help you to maintain a "heavenly home" while you have a full-time job outside the home.

Success in the home is of utmost importance. You, too, can make it — even though you work!

viii

Chapter One

Keeping Up Your Self-Image

How did you feel this morning when you left home? Were you in high spirits? Happy and cheerful? Were you all set for an interesting day on the job? Or was it an effort to get things together? Were you dreading another day at the "salt mine"? Did you have so much to do that you didn't know where to start?

Are you one of those working women who's always wondering: "What on earth is the matter with me? I can't *get* going anymore, let alone keep going. I feel like a complete failure. I can't keep house properly. I'm always tired and grouchy. I'm bored with my job."

Take another look — at yourself, and the situation you find yourself in.

Take heart. You're not alone. Many women are finding it necessary to work full-time while juggling the myriad duties of marriage, home, children, and church. Frances N. Boyden describes the feeling:

"A terrible sense of inadequacy comes over me when I ponder the fact that I am attempting to do so many things, play so many roles . . . in my daily life! . . . And I realize that all women are playing many roles. I see in my daily life the continual challenge to fill many needs. But with the challenge comes problems of balance, of perspective and of changing responsibilities.

"All women have the same challenge, the same need to function in many roles. Each person marches to a different drummer, but every one of us finds herself with a variety of roles to play simultaneously."[1]

While it helps to know you are not alone in one sense, you must also realize that you are *you*. And, as Mrs. Boyden noted, "each person marches to a different drummer." In this sense, you are alone. You're unlike any other person. You are different. Your talents vary. So does your sense of organization, your goals, your likes, and your dislikes. You are not alone in that you have many different roles to play; but you are alone in how you perform those roles. You cannot compare how you cope with how your neighbor copes. You cannot compare accomplishments or failures. Only you can decide how you will handle your job, your family, your pressures, your secret desires, and your ambitions.

2

If you accept this, you can learn to be happy with yourself. You can learn to like yourself. Your self-image is of utmost importance if you are to succeed as a wife, a homemaker, and a mother in the limited time available to a working woman.

Take a long, hard look at yourself. Why aren't you enjoying yourself? Do you have any real troubles? If so, do something about them. Change the things that can be changed, and accept calmly those things that cannot be changed.

Ask yourself: Am I building for eternity? Or, am I even building?

Could it be that you are stagnating in a rut? A rut that says

[1]Frances N. Boyden, "The Many Lives of Women," *The Joy of Being a Woman,* compiled by Duane and Jean Crowther (Horizon Publishers, Bountiful, Utah), 1972, p. 281.

you can't be creative, you can't grow, "because you work." You needn't be.

Look at each day as a new adventure, a time to mold and build. Don't ever let things become monotonous. Find a new challenge every day.

Your Very Own Treasure

What's the most valuable treasure you have? Your family. If you had a valuable gemstone, wouldn't you find time to refine and polish it? Wouldn't it be worth taking care of?

So it is with your "treasure." You have to lay up your treasure "where moth and rust will not corrupt." Your most valuable possession is your family, for it is the joy of eternity. The added responsibility of a job away from home does not lessen the load as far as your family is concerned. But it does give you the opportunity to refine your ability to cope and adjust and schedule.

3

Make the effort to polish and refine the treasures your Heavenly Father has given you.

Oh, yes, it takes work and effort; but that is where you, as wife and/or mother, come in. You have to go the second mile, then the third. Remember, it's you who sets the mood, the tone, and the feeling. A mother's or wife's lilting spirit is contagious.

I attended a workshop at Brigham Young University, where the speaker advised staff members to "sparkle from eight to five. . . not eight to twelve or eight to three, but eight to five." She said, "We should take every short opportunity we have to refresh ourselves, so that we really sparkle all day." Inwardly I moaned, "Sure!" The thought, however, bothered me. It kept finding its way back into my thinking. Finally I decided to try it. Only I was going to "sparkle" for my family — after five, in those few precious hours I have with them. I was amazed at the difference. When I put on a "happy face," I soon felt happy; and it didn't take long to see how happy my family was. I still slip into the comfortable rut of not putting forth any more effort than absolutely necessary. But, as soon as I recognize the slip, I try again. It really is worth the effort. When I "sparkle," my family "sparkles"; and my burdens seem lighter.

No Time for Self-Pity

How you feel about yourself *does matter*! You can hear something a thousand times, but you still have to prove it for yourself. You have to make it work, or it has no value.

If you have to work, accept the fact, try to enjoy it, and then try to manage your time better. Make the best possible use of what time you have.

Put your best self forward. Your husband and your children are the most important people in your life, more so than all the "important" contacts and clients on the job.

4

You worry about your husband, your children, their problems, and your problems. *Maybe it's time to stop thinking and do something.* What better place to start than with yourself. The whole atmosphere of your home revolves around "ME," "I," "YOU," the woman, the mother, the wife.

No matter how glad your children and husband are to see you at the end of the day, their mood will be quickly dampened if you are tired and grouchy. Your few hours together will be tainted by moments of selfish thinking and acting.

Struggle to overcome how you feel and consider how your family feels. Try to see the "other side of the fence." Remember, your family has waited all day long to see you, to unload their problems, to share their experiences, to tell their needs. They need time for the countless things they "have to" talk about and solve — right now. They need "Mom, the mother," not "Mom, the tired working gal," or "Honey, the wife," not "Mrs. Smith, the tired office slave." Supplying this need may be difficult to do, but it can become a habit. Listening strengthens family bonds. Take a fifteen- or twenty-minute break. Sit down and listen to your family's adventures as you unwind. The rewards will be a happier, stronger family.

Don't worry about not having more time to spend with them. Make the most of the time you have by improving your mental attitude. Enjoy today, instead of just waiting for the day you can quit your job.

Remember, discouragement, depression, and self-pity *do not* come from a good source.

Try not to consider yourself a martyr. Give yourself the opportunity to progress and grow in the role of mother, wife, and woman — while also growing in your job. Your time schedule varies considerably from that of the "everyday housewife." When setting goals, remember you are actually working two full-time jobs. You have the responsibilities of both home and job. Don't be discouraged if you don't reach objectives as quickly and as often as you would expect if you were home all day.

5

Keep That Special Spark

Here are some suggestions to help you think about who you are and what you are, deep down inside. They will help you keep the spark that makes *you* special.

Give yourself half an hour at the end of the day to unwind — do nothing but think, fantasize, or whatever.

Take a walk in the fresh air, even around the block, to appreciate the big beautiful world outside the four walls at work and the four walls at home.

Organize your life. Get up a little earlier, so you leave your house feeling good. Never forget to kiss your husband and children good-by before you leave.

Get enough rest for both your mental and physical health. But don't try to sleep away your problems. Sometimes a task completed is more restful than another hour's sleep.

Learn to relax while you are at home. Enjoy your blessings. Unbend from the rigid schedule. Remember, your chores will wait, but the joys of having your family about you can pass you by.

Take a few minutes each night to evaluate what you have accomplished that day. You will be surprised at how many things you have done. Don't overlook the small things; they all add up.

Turn your "fridge" door into a "poster" — your spot of "refreshment." Clip and tape items, thoughts, poems, jokes, a poignant picture — anything to lift your spirits and encourage you to keep going. For three years, my poster included poems, sayings, and — prominently displayed — the floor plan for my dream house.

6

Look for the good and beautiful in all things, all places, and all people, no matter what your situation. If you work in a factory, see the beauty in design and pattern. If you are in an office with a window, enjoy the changing beauty outside. Take a lunch-break walk and look for things your eyes may have missed before. Enjoy the goodness of people around you. Be aware of others.

Keep a *positive* attitude. Count *all* your blessings, and be thankful.

A Little Exercise Will Help

Your self-image deteriorates rapidly if you aren't feeling good physically. That tired, ache-all-over feeling may signal the need for a physical-fitness effort, especially if your job is particularly confining. Find some way to get in a little exercise. It will help keep your blood circulating and your mind active and clear. It isn't necessary to schedule an exercise period during those valuable hours at home.

Take advantage of exercise opportunities at work, and you'll feel fit and alive when you get home.

If you have an office errand to run, don't use the elevator. Take the stairs. Of course, you'll use wisdom. If you aren't used to climbing stairs, start by walking up one flight and taking the elevator the rest of the way. Coming down, walk two flights and ride the rest. Challenge yourself to be able to climb four flights within two months — without having a total collapse at the top.

Don't spend your break sitting with your feet up. Take a brisk walk for part of it, then sit with your feet up. Work at it until you enjoy walking during the whole break. This serves two purposes. A change of scenery refreshes your mind, and the activity stimulates your body.

Perhaps your working environment does not lend to taking walks outside of the building. Is there an area inside that you could "tour"?

7

If walking inside the building is impossible, the women's rest room and lounge can be a last resort. Take a few minutes to jog in place, do ten jumping jacks, and touch your toes ten times. You can offer your own explanations when someone discovers you.

I once worked in an office with one other secretary. Our boss was gone most of the time. It became an enjoyable break-time habit to lock the doors and jog around our desks for five or ten minutes. Usually we ended up laughing as we visualized the looks and kidding we would get if our boss returned. But, we felt better.

A few minutes' exercise will give you the energy needed to keep going.

Look the Part

How you look is of utmost importance to your self-image. The day you leave the house looking drab and thrown-together is the day you'll start wondering about your own worth. By the time you get back home, you'll be tired and grouchy. So take the time to make sure you look your best. Choose a hairstyle that's easy to care for, and it will always look nice. Pamper yourself with manicures. And don't forget makeup. A little eye shadow and mascara give you a wide-awake look, even if you don't feel wide-awake. And, a touch of color on your cheeks adds a healthy glow.

Then of course, you'll want to dress attractively. Clothing you wear to work should be appropriate for your job. This usually means something simple — not elaborate or gaudy, not dull or drab.

Clothes. An extensive working wardrobe could easily devour your hard-earned paychecks. And, since you no longer have the time to shop the sales or sew as much as you would like, you must be doubly earnest in seeking cost-cutting ways to dress well. Try some of these suggestions to stretch your clothing budget and get the "most for your money."

Invest wisely, considering both quality and variety. Quality clothes, while they cost more, wear longer. When buying basic styles and colors, invest in quality. Add variety with less expensive items. For instance, splurge on a good skirt or a quality pantsuit, but buy less expensive blouses. And, if you go for novelty or fad items, choose the less expensive ones so you won't feel badly when they are no longer in style.

Choose separates whenever possible. Skirts and blouses or pants and tops give you a greater variety. Choose several items in a neutral color, then dress them up with bright, cheerful colors which will lift your spirits and help to create a happy atmosphere around you. Start with a color scheme — usually only two basic colors — and stick to it. One or two novelty items are fine, but the majority should be basic. Create your own schemes. By doing so

8

you can save money. If you purchase matched sets, add another top or two, or a skirt, to extend the versatility of the outfit. Consider:

— Pantsuits. Vary tops, blouses, jackets, vests, sweaters, or a combination of these.
— Sweaters. Select cardigans, pullovers, and turtlenecks. Try crocheting or knitting your own.
— Jackets. Choose from a variety of long-sleeved and short-sleeved; tailored and casual; and plain colors, prints, checks and plaids.
— Vests, ponchos, stoles. Vary styles, materials and colors.

Accessories. Change your outfit to meet the moment. Inexpensive accessories can turn a plain skirt and blouse or a basic dress into a snappy, fashionable outfit. They provide the finishing touches and make the costume distinctly yours. The trick is not being afraid to try. Be daring. When shopping for accessories, don't overlook your local discount store or "five and ten."

— Scarves are magical wardrobe extenders. They come in many designs and shapes. When an outfit seems drab, tie on a bright scarf. Experiment with different ways to wear them — tied in a bow, flowing, tucked in, fastened with a pin. A scarf tied in a perky manner around your head may be just the lift you and your hairdo need. A bright color next to your face is usually flattering.
— Belts can also lend a splash of color or a touch of personality for a needed change. You can choose knitted, crocheted, beaded, chains, leather, macrame, cords. They can be bright or subtle, suitable for many outfits.
— Jewelry selections are endless. Choose carefully for the job. Jewelry should not be "gobby" or get in the way. Pins are delightful and definitely add personality to your total appearance. They can be formal, pretty, or just cute. Simple necklaces and bracelets also add

9

to the total effect. And don't forget rings. Wear them judiciously, but wear them. The flash and sparkle you see can boost your spirits.

— Purses and shoes can be colorful and make a complete change in the appearance of a costume.

A word about shoes. While shoes can serve as an accessory, be practical. Health and comfort is high on the priority list when it comes to working all day or all night — especially if you are on your feet most of the time. You lose your "sparkle" quickly if you have tired, aching legs and feet. You need shoes that support your feet and legs.

To pacify vanity keep a good, comfortable pair of shoes at work and wear the glamour pair to and from work.

Different styles of clothing and accessories completely change the appearance of an outfit.

10   Building for Eternity

Keep up your self-image. Remember that you are you, and you are a very important person. You have a valuable mission, that of building an eternal family. And how well you will succeed depends on how well you care for yourself. Work constantly to build up that self-image, mentally and physically.

Chapter Two

Maintaining Togetherness

When you work, the task of keeping the family unit secure and maintaining a happy attitude sometimes seems an insurmountable chore. But, if you put your mind to it and plan ahead, you can do it.

Remember, your attitude as the mother and wife sets the mood for the whole family. The atmosphere you create carries them and yourself through the day.

The key to a happy, secure family is love. Let them know at all times how much you love and appreciate them.

When my children were small, I started a game that I shall always be grateful for. I knew the time would come when my son or daughter might not like a display of affection. But, I wanted to be able to let them know at any time of my great love for them.

The game started as a bedtime exchange. I tucked each of them in, asking, "You know what?" Each would reply, "What?" Then I would say, "I sure do love you." This went on for a long time, until their comeback became "Yes, Momma, I know. You love me." Then I changed my tactics. I'd say, "No, that's not right. I love you the 'mostest'." Soon they picked it up, and the fun began. We would playfully argue about who loved whom the very "most-est." Soon the hall would echo. "I do." "No sir, I do." "No, I do." "I DO." This loving, delightful family "feud" has carried through the years. Now, as my son leaves with friends for a scout meeting, all I have to say is "I do." With his ornery grin, he replies, "Naw, I do." But he knows. My daughter and I "argue" all the time. It's such a delight to have her run down the block trying to call back the last "I do." She knows.

Since I have had to work, just being able to say "I do" has spanned a lot of gaps.

Start Each Day Right

Start the day right — together. Even though it's rushed and hectic, it can be happy.

12

Breakfast is a good time to review the day's schedule — not only chores to be done, but meetings, appointments, activities. It also gives you a chance to see what kind of clothes are being worn that day, especially if the children are at an age where they need to be checked. If they are older, why pass up an opportunity to make them feel good? Perhaps the boost they need for the day will be when you take the time to tell them how attractive they look or how nice they smell.

It's a nice habit to wish everyone a good day. "Have a nice day" means a lot when it comes from Mom.

Once in a while, when it is especially beautiful outside or smells particularly fresh and sweet, get everyone up early and rush them outside, so they can be excited about how wonderful the world is. They may consider you a bit crazy, but they'll probably humor you. The spirit is catching. In time, they will call you to see the moon peep through the clouds, just because "I knew you'd like it."

An early-morning "sparkle" may be difficult to achieve; but, remember, your attitude reflects on everyone.

Whenever I feel a case of morning blahs coming on, I pull out a well-worn clipping. Rereading this mother's experience never fails to perk me up.

"At the breakfast table one morning, our teen-age son brought me up short with the remark, 'What's the matter today, has everyone taken grouch pills?'

" 'What do you mean by that?' I asked with a hint of annoyance in my voice.

" 'Well, I don't know what's happened,' he answered, 'but it's sure like a morgue around here.'

" 'Grouch pills.' 'Like a morgue.' These words were quite an indictment for any home. Could it be that I was responsible for this atmosphere?

" 'I think I do as well as most of my friends, ' I rationalized to myself after everyone had left for work or school. 'I try to be a good mother, keep the house clean, the clothes washed and ironed, cook nutritious meals. Where am I falling short? Am I failing to create for my family a cheerful atmosphere that will radiate beyond the walls of our home?'

13

"It was then I decided to try a little secret experiment, a little disguised campaign to improve the situation, and being a musician, I turned to music as my tool. My strategy was simple. Each morning as I prepared breakfast, put up the lunches, and got my family ready for the day's work, I would deliberately hum a little tune, or quietly sing a song. I was well aware that there would be some days when I just wouldn't feel like any kind of a song, but I was determined to give my experiment a try.

"Nothing happened for some time, and just as I had about decided that maybe my idea wasn't such a good one after all, the payoff came. When my son left the breakfast table one morning, he said enthusiastically: 'Gee, Mom, that was a good breakfast. What's for dinner tonight?' And he went out of the door whistling the melody I had had such a struggle to sing that morning.

"Then my husband remarked, as he picked up the car keys and prepared to leave, 'I don't know what's happened, Honey, but things seem to be going a lot smoother lately.' He left the house humming the same tune.

" 'Maybe my little experiment does work,' I said to myself, hardly daring to believe what I had just heard.

"I quickly cleared the table and washed up the dishes, and then, all of sudden, grinned sheepishly as I realized that I, too, was unconsciously humming the tune I had sung earlier.

" 'What do you know?' I said, aloud this time. 'It works both ways. I guess I'm a victim of my own experiment.' "[1]

14 The Secret of Keeping in Touch

Even though you can't be with your family all you would like to be, you can let them know — often when they least expect it — that you are thinking about them. Write secret messages and leave them to be found when they will do the most good. Tuck a "love" note into a textbook, a pocket, a purse. My husband often opens his briefcase to find a note saying "I'm thinking of you," or "Hi," or just the small face that has become my signature ☺ .

A recipe for lunch. If your family carries sack lunches, slip in a paper napkin with a silly drawing, a funny face, or just a "Hi." If it's holiday time, draw an Easter egg, a jack-o'-lantern, or a Christmas tree. Occasionally, slip in a note reminding them of an important "date" — with you at dinner.

A boiled egg can serve the same purpose. Draw or write on the shell with a felt-tip pen. Presto! Instant love shows up in the form of a boiled egg.

[1]Wilma Boyle Bunker, "Morning Melody", *The Relief Society Magazine* (Salt Lake City, Utah, April 1967), p. 290.

You can even use the space on the outside of a lunch bag. Not everyone has a personalized lunch sack. They can be fun to fix and fun to carry. A bit of amateur artwork can convey a multitude of important messages — especially that all-important message, "I care." Very few lunches leave our house without some joke, drawing, or comment somewhere in or on it. My own lunch bag often makes a tour of the office after my children and the felt-tip pens or crayons have been at work.

Filling the empty echo. Many young people say the worst part of the day is coming home to an empty, echoing house. If your children are old enough to be alone when you're not there, you can help fill the emptiness with a little thought and little effort. It only takes a note propped on the table or a pillow, a treat, or a picture.

Almost anything can be a reminder that says "I care." Perhaps a short note saying, "Hi, did you have a nice day?" or "I'll be home in a little while — I just wanted you to know that I was thinking about you." You may have to leave instructions on chores to be done, but once in a while note things they *don't* have to do. "Today, you don't have to clean the trash can with a toothbrush." "Don't worry about washing the ceiling today, we can do it the second Tuesday of next week." It only takes a minute of your time now to bring smiles to their faces later. And, it creates an enjoyable atmosphere to come home to. You'll look forward to seeing what their reaction was.

15

On a special occasion, you might even leave a note telling them to turn on the tape recorder. Your voice could then fill the emptiness with a joke, a song, or a happy thought.

Once in a while put a candy bar on the bed with a note attached, "After your exhausting day at school, here's some energy to help you get through until dinnertime." Or, "Please get the alligator steak out to thaw for snack."

All the little things add up to a big difference.

One short phone call. What about the day your children have somewhere special to go after school or parts in a program? You are not there to offer the last-minute helps. But maybe you could find a few minutes for a *short* telephone call. Tell them to have a good time, and ask them to remember all the good things that happen so they can tell you just as soon as you get home. Wish them luck. A loving word is almost as good as a pat on the back. (Of course, you will be considerate of the office or working conditions where you are employed and not take advantage of a situation.)

In some working situations, you might be able to use your afternoon break for a phone call home. One woman said this solved the problem of her not being there when her daughter came home. "I would insist that she always call me when she got home. Then I would take time away from my work to listen. This was my break for the afternoon." If you choose this option, clear it with your boss first. And it would be a good idea to let your co-workers know of the arrangement to avoid any hard feelings.

A Sharing Time

The evening meal can become the time for sharing the fun and the laughs of the day. Allow everyone his fair share of time. And insist that each one listen to the others' "happenings." This should not be a time of confusion or rivalry. If something has gone rather badly for one, try to use it as a teaching and learning experience for the others.

Try to leave your job problems and pressures at work. They will be polite and wait there for you. You don't need to burden your family with them. Once in a while, if you have older children, you may ask their advice about a particular problem. Give heed to their suggestions, then report back the results. Don't underestimate your offspring.

16

Family Affairs

Learn to take time to enjoy your family. It's easy to get caught in the routine of trying to get everything done because you "don't have enough time." One young woman expressed the thought well. "It isn't as much a matter of having more time to spend with them [your family], as it is improving your mental attitude so you enjoy today, instead of just waiting for the day you'll have more time."

Plan family activities, then give them the same rank and importance that any other meetings or obligations have — or higher. Never postpone or cancel these activities, except for a real emergency. When your time is limited because of the hours you spend on the job, your children and husband need to know their desires and hopes are as important as anything else on your calendar. A child can take the disappointment of being "canceled out" only so many times. Developing confidence and love cannot be done with too many disappointments.

17

Add a "Kid's Day" to your calendar. A real authentic holiday, just like Mother's Day and Father's Day. On Kid's Day, *they* can choose the menu and activities (within reason and your budget). Spend the day together. Let your children see how important they are.

Some of the most enjoyable family affairs can be strictly spur-of-the-moment.

I think it's great to come home and say, "Forget supper for now, we'll open a can of soup later. Let's go and walk in the leaves." So we drink a cup of soup at nine. We have had fun — leaf fights, crunching leaves, smelling the marvelous autumn air. And, with rosy cheeks and happy hearts, we fall into our beds and sleep well.

I recall one Saturday the weather had been quite ferocious — thunder, lightning, and pouring rain. In the afternoon, the sun finally broke through. That was the signal for the children to go outside. Soon, my son and daughter came running in. "Come and help us, Momma. Hurry, come and help us." I dropped what I was doing and rushed outside. "What's the matter? What's wrong?" "Look in the puddles, Mom? See them? We can't get them out fast enough. C'mon, hurry. They're drowning! C'mon, Mom."

I spent two enjoyable hours rescuing earthworms with my two children.

It only has to start to be a good rainstorm now, and they laugh, "Hey, Mom, remember that day. . . ."

Another thing that we enjoy as a family is a "car picnic." This usually occurs on a Saturday when Dad says, "Let's go." Obviously, nothing is planned or organized. We go to the cupboard and the nearest store to pick out a few "nibble foods," such as cheese and crackers, apples or oranges, and a can of soda pop or juice for each of us. Then with our goodies packed in the car, we drive until we find a place we would like to explore. It could be a new store, a park, a neighboring city, a beach or a canyon. If possible, we eat outside; if not, we eat our picnic in the car.

One of our car picnics was in the middle of the winter. We ate in the car; and we played Frisbee on frozen Utah Lake.

The Communication Connection

An effective communication system is essential to a strong family unit. No matter how big or how small a problem may seem, talk it over with your family. They might see it in an entirely different light. As you bring problems before the children and listen to their ideas and solutions, they begin to realize that you too have problems. Then, they will feel comfortable discussing things that have been bothering them. (Of course, there are personal problems that you as an adult should not discuss with an immature youth.) The idea is, even though you are Mom and Dad,

18

you still have problems. If you consider their ideas when solving some of these problems, you will go a long way in forming a close-knit family.

We have made it a habit on family night to specifically ask each person, in turn, if they have a problem that needs to be discussed. When I first went back to work, it seemed I had the most problems to solve. Our family night discussions helped my children to gain understanding. They learned to see how I felt about things, and that I could cry because I felt badly. I also came to realize the scope of understanding my family possessed.

Since you must work and be away from the family a great deal, you need to communicate your love in as many ways as possible. Doesn't it make you feel "special" when a friend does something nice, "just because"? Thoughtful little things are important to your husband and children. They become "tokens of love."

19

For example, one week my son and daughter worked extremely hard to clean the house, doing many tasks besides their regular chores. They did this to please me, so I wouldn't have to do them when I got home. They did it to show me how much they loved me. One day towards the end of the week, I took part of my lunch hour to buy each of them a small trinket to go on the collection shelves in their rooms. Since I was at work, I had no fancy wrapping paper or ribbon. I took a small piece of scratch paper and wrote with a felt-tip pen:

"I love you, and I really appreciate all you do!"

I drew hearts all over the paper, wrapped the trinket in it, and fastened it with a rubber band. I put these "presents" on their beds where they would find them later. The glow on their faces matched the glow in my heart.

There have been times when my husband was having a particularly hard time studying a certain subject and when I delighted in getting his textbooks and writing my interpretation of the subject in the margin for him to find when he got up before dawn to study some more.

This kind of communication is a vital part of our family life. It isn't a difficult habit to form, and the rewards are many.

Look for the Joys That Are There

With such limited time at home, concentrate on all that is good. Try to find joy, rather than faults. It isn't hard to find faults; they are rather obvious. I haven't found a shy fault yet. You don't have to look for them; they find you. But, you can create a better attitude which will reflect in the total mood of the home if you are consciously looking for things that are good and happy. Take time to laugh with your children, thoroughly enjoy them. It's such fun to see a personality and sense of humor grow. What a joy when you are able to recognize a spark of spiritual strength. Will you see it if you are looking elsewhere — or not looking at all?

Our family is a great one for teasing. It's such fun to be able to play as a family.

Our son is a typical boy. If we remind him to take a bath on Thursday, his answer is usually something like, "Why? I had one last Saturday, and I'll have to take one again this Saturday for church. Who needs two baths that close together?"

One evening, Erin had been reminded several times to get washed for dinner. Still, he came to the table with smudges on his face. "Erin, did you wash?" I asked. "Sure, Mom."

"If you washed, what is that on your face?" Promptly, and in all sincerity, he answered, "I don't know. What color is it?"

Felt-tip pens and construction paper are valuable assets at our house. We constantly make one another cards, notes and drawings. This has been extended to include friends

20

and relatives. We seldom use "store-bought" cards. It means so much more to receive a poem or verse written just for you. One Mother's Day card from my son was a large piece of construction paper, with yarn fastened to each end so it could be strung across the kitchen doorway. It said: "Mother, stay out of the kitchen today. Have a happy Mother's Day. I love you." No store-bought card could compare to that.

It makes my day to come home from work to find my bed made and a note scribbled on a small scrap of paper. "I love you. I hope you weren't too late for work."

In my office window I keep a small rock painted with red, white, and blue stripes. Lettered in gold across the front are the words, *I Love You*. Right next to it sits a small, yellow crocheted pillow stuffed with tissue paper. The pillow has *I Love You* sewn on it. These are gentle reminders of my children's love for me, "so you won't be lonely and miss us too much."

21

Do you know what a joy it is to have breakfast in bed on Saturday morning, "so you can rest on your day off"? How delicious the cold toast and cold hot chocolate taste! Never before have cold, peppered, scrambled eggs been so elegant.

How long has it been since you and your family have gone for a walk to see what you could find in the field or empty lot? Maybe you need to take a walk to find the empty lot. There is so much beauty and activity to be discovered and shared. Take time to pause and watch the teeming life among the blades of grass. If you live in the city, discover the beauty in structures, shapes, and shadows.

Don't get caught in the rut of working, coming home, and collapsing. If you do, you will miss some of life's greatest opportunities. Your family and the happiness of being will pass you by. It takes so little effort, even when you are tired from having been at work all day. Be aware of what is happening around you. Do you know what spring smells like? Can you recall how long it takes for the tiny, baby green leaves to become full and cover the bare trees? How many shades of orange are there when autumn comes? What is your youngest daughter's favorite color — this week?

There is joy just around the corner, waiting for you to discover it, share it, and give it.

FAMILY TRADITIONS

Some of the greatest and strongest ties are family traditions. What a tremendous opportunity for you to build strength and solidarity in your family. Make traditions a high priority. Since you must be away from home a great deal, make the time spent with the family meaningful and remembered. Traditions are the building blocks of memories.

22

Let me share a few of my own family's traditions with you. Maybe an idea will appeal to you and can be worked into your schedule.

Family Night Candles

Family night is one evening a week that is set aside to be spent with the family. Sometimes we study together, sometimes it's an activity night. Since our children were small, we've had a special way of beginning family night. We eat our evening meal by candlelight. On holidays, it is a special candle; other times any candle will do, sometimes two. Some of the candles we have enjoyed the most are "modernistic," thanks to shaping by the sun. Any menu becomes special by candlelight. Try it and see how elegant hot dogs and beans can be.

Birthdays

Birthdays are always special days. Each person gets to choose the menus for his day. When they awaken on "their morning," they find balloons taped up all over the house. Usually there is a large hand-drawn banner. If we can afford it, we put up crepe paper streamers. On my last birthday, we had the most beautiful streamers that we have ever had. I came home to find the drapes drawn and the door locked. As I unlocked the door, my husband and children shouted, "Surprise! Surprise!" The living room and dining room looked like a huge blue-yarn spider web, full of balloons. Perched on top of a curtain rod was the remainder of a ball of yarn, still attached. It was beautiful.

We try to get up early on birthdays so we can have breakfast together and open at least one present.

In the evening, we have our "special" supper, even though it might be macaroni and cheese. Then comes the cake and ice cream. We usually try to share that with Grandma.

Pumpkin Hunting

23

What a great time of year fall is! Several weeks before Halloween, we start pumpkin hunting. Being city folks most of our lives, we haven't grown our own. We look, weigh, hold, thump, measure, and plan. It has become tradition that we each have a jack-o'-lantern. One year when the budget was tighter than usual, we had the choice of an "almost large" pumpkin for the whole family or a very tiny one for each of us. We voted for the tiny ones. That year we tried to outdo each other to see who could find the tiniest one. It had to be a pumpkin, not a squash or gourd. Each year, we spend days talking about the shape and kind of face we want. The Saturday prior to the family night before Halloween is pumpkin day. We find "the ones" and lovingly take them home. Then on family night, we create our superb jack-o'-lanterns.

Pillow House

When someone is sick, I have a special way to say I love you. I build them a pillow house. If they have to remain in bed, that's where the pillow house is made. If they can stay on the couch, that's the construction site. I gather up every pillow in the house. I use them for building blocks, making sure the most comfortable ones are behind the individual. The fancy, frilly ones are part of the wall farthest away, so nothing is spilled on them. It's not how many pillows you have that counts, it's the fact that you care enough to do something special. The pillow house offers cozy, soft security in a temporary world of aches and sneezes.

One of the hardest things I had to do when I began working was to leave my children when they were ill. This one tradition has helped me help them. I build a pillow house, then call often to check on them.

Fourth of July

24

On the Fourth we have to have a picnic, with a watermelon. We try to find a parade to watch. As evening comes, we find the best place to sit and watch the fireworks. It is usually a happy, fun-filled, hot day — not too different from everyone else's Fourth.

Christmas

What a precious, beautiful time of year Christmas is!

We start scheming and planning in October. What will our gifts be this year for Grandma and Grandpa? What can we make for them? Our secret projects require much discussion and thought. We always take on too many projects, and there's always something we don't quite get done. But, it's well worth the effort. We talk about the person we are making the gift for, as it grows and progresses. "Will he like it?" "Grandma will like it no matter what it is, just because we made it."

Over the years, I have seen my children develop creative talents as well as an understanding and love for other people. They have grown in their desire to give.

Many of our pre-Christmas family nights are spent "making things," as are most Saturdays during that period.

If you try the do-it-yourself route, preplan your work activities. If you have older children, they can prepare a light meal, such as soup and sandwiches. As soon as everyone is home, you can eat and get to work. Get out your project supplies in the morning before you leave for work, or even the night before. Depending on how many projects you plan to undertake, start several weeks or months ahead. That way, it won't become a hectic, tiring rush; it will remain an enjoyable family activity.

The other family. We have tried to teach our family to have a special attitude about giving — to have a desire to give and help, as much as to receive.

Every year, we have tried to find a family to share our love. We provide as much Christmas for them as we possibly can. At our family council, we discuss how much we have to spend on Christmas. We consider ways we can trim our own "lists" so we'll have something extra to share with our "other family." We talk about it, and then ask for a vote.

25

It is so much fun to make and buy and bake and wrap — all in secret, for we never sign a card or tell the family who the gift is from. Now that our children are older, they have the joy of putting the box on the doorstep, ringing the bell, and running.

The tree. Our tree can't be an ordinary tree. It has to be a special tree, because it is "our tree." After Thanksgiving when the tree lots start springing up, we snatch a few minutes here and there to wander through the lots just to smell the delightful aroma. When we lived in California, we always had "Tree Day" two Saturdays before Christmas. We packed a picnic lunch and went into the mountains, to specified areas where we could tromp over the mountainsides until we found "the one." If we had parked at the top of the canyon, we could be assured of finding our tree at the bottom, and vice versa.

Since moving to Utah, we have found it almost as much fun to become the best bargain hunters in the county, going from lot to lot picking and choosing.

We always decorate our tree during family night the week before Christmas.

Decorations. Our decorations have become traditions too. We always have an old-fashioned tree. Some of the ornaments belonged to the children's great-grandfather. One or two are heirlooms from Germany. Every year we make something new to hang on the tree. When we bring out the boxes, we find not only lights and bulbs, but treasures and memories. Paper and popcorn chains are a must.

"My own tree." Somehow we always manage to salvage several of the large branches that have to be trimmed off the bottom of the tree. Each child takes a branch for "my own tree." The trees are taken to each bedroom and decorated. The children are allowed to use some lights and decorations, but they usually end up making a lot more. They each have to keep "their tree" watered and cared for.

Christmas Eve. Our most meaningful and special night of the year is Christmas Eve. We have a birthday party, with cake and ice cream, to celebrate the birth of Jesus. We start our program by reading several traditional Christmas stories. We recall the many legends about the beginnings of Christmas traditions. Then we read the scriptures about the Christ Child and the first Christmas. As these are read, the children put the figures into the nativity scene. And, of course, we sing all our favorite carols. Then we cut the cake and sing "Happy Birthday," so we might remember whose birthday it is we celebrate, why the first gifts were given, and that they were brought with love.

The goodies. Christmas wouldn't be Christmas without certain cookies and breads. We bake together and deco-

26

rate cookies together. We even enjoy eating the cookie dough together. We've made it part of our holiday tradition to bake small breads and fancy cookies. Some of these are put on paper plates and wrapped as presents. Early on Christmas Eve, we take these plates to the homes of our neighbors and close friends. When the door is answered, we sing a carol, give them their goodies, and go on our way.

Form Your Own Traditions

Traditions are formed by what you and your family enjoy doing, so you will want to do it again and again. It doesn't have to be elaborate or expensive. It only has to belong to your family. If you stop and think about it, you may be surprised at many traditions you already have. The important thing for you to remember, while you are working and not at home as much as you would like to be, is that these kinds of traditions will help hold your family together. Start now; it's never too late to build family traditions.

27

Chapter Three

Sharing Responsibilities

When Mother must work, she must have cooperation and help to maintain a properly functioning home. M-A-R-T-Y-R does not spell mother. You don't have to be the only one to do housework and other necessary tasks.

As one mother wisely said, "We should all work together caring for our home and each other." This is a good attitude. It is the family's home. We *are* caring for each other. Take time when you're home to have your children work with you. This not only develops a good work ethic, but it also makes the children feel the care of the house is as much their job as it is Mother's.

You are not being truly kind if you do not allow your children to learn the reality and responsibility of work. Train your children to do their share of the household duties. It helps you as the mother, but it also helps them grow into responsible, considerate adults.

Sometimes, we wonder just how much help they really are. Wilma M. Despain expresses the feeling in her poem, "For His Tomorrows."

His own boat, a cardboard box,
His playroom is a deep blue sea.

He catches fish (his own small sox),
My best broom is a tall palm tree.

But now, "I'll help you Mommy —
I'll clean the house and dust it, see!"
I wouldn't have him know for worlds
How much his help is hindering me.[1]

Having children help doesn't mean they should assume all the responsibilities. However, they need to learn the satisfaction that comes with a sense of accomplishment.

Our young people need to be praised, to feel needed and worthwhile. It doesn't take much effort (even if you are tired) to say: "Thank you," "I surely appreciate your help," "That certainly looks nice now," or "It's so good to have someone who cares enough to help me when I get home." Of course you know, it takes fewer muscles and less exertion to say it with a smile than with a frown.

29

Remember, these young individuals residing in your home are children who are learning. They are *not* perfectionists. Usually their motto is, "the fastest way is the 'bestest' way." In their realm of thinking, they don't realize Mom might not agree. Be firm, but gentle. Children need standards to reach for. But they should be secure in the knowledge that, if they miss half the dust bunnies in the morning, Mom will still love them when she gets home in the evening. The next time you assign the task, take a minute or two to explain how it should be done.

During the time you have at home, there are tasks that must be done. If you can turn the chores into games, the children will be anxious to help. You can help them to realize that if the dishes get done fast, you can enjoy more time together.

[1]Wilma M. Despain, "For His Tomorrows" (*The Relief Society Magazine*, Salt Lake City, Utah, December 1970), p. 930.

In giving children the responsibility of chores, you have given yourself the opportunity to develop such hidden talents as intuition, perception, and great wisdom. If your house is anything like ours, these talents will develop very rapidly — out of necessity. You will have to use them to find the new hiding places your children have found for the utensils and everyday bowls. These caches have been discovered since the last time the dishes were put away. (Was that only last night?) It's amazing how, in only six drawers and a few cupboards, things manage to disappear.

If someone ever designs a "sleuthing" course for working mothers whose children do the dishes and other chores, I will be the first to enroll.

Cooking

I had told both of my children that as soon as they were big enough to pick up a pan from the top of the stove, without being injured, I would teach them to cook. This can be a great boon to the working mother, and it presents a lot of opportunities for the children. Even small children can prepare simple parts of a meal. As they get older, they can help more and more. Soon they may even surprise you with "dinner on the table."

Sandi at 10½ was being kind and loving. Without being asked, she prepared a pancake supper. All through the meal she kept asking, "Are they all right? Do they taste okay?" Finally, I took the hint and said, "Yes, they taste all right. Why?" A sweet smile lit up her face. "I just wondered. I couldn't find enough flour, so I used cornstarch instead. I hoped they would be all right."

After several years of practice, she is now an excellent cook.

Chore Charts

If your children have trouble remembering what chores

they have to do and when, make up a weekly chore chart.

We have lots of fun with chore charts at our house. We use construction paper and a felt-tip pen. Any piece of paper will work, as long as it is large enough to contain all the information you want on it. Change the charts regularly so the children can alternate their responsibilities. Be creative in designing the chart, so it doesn't become a permanent fixture to be ignored. A chore chart that changes often, with a special note or joke from Mom, will encourage a lot more cooperation than nagging or threats.

CHORE CHART SUGGESTIONS

— Vary shape and color
— Vary chores to be done (these should be according to age and capabilities)
— Draw fun sketches or cartoons (not professional, of course)
— Write a happy note on it
— Pin on paper awards
  Such as: "Creates Improvement in This Room for First Time in a Century!"
  "Best Looking Floor in the House"
— Award a "Bonus Stamp"
  Sometimes, put a "bonus stamp" in the lower right corner. This stamp may be removed at the end of a specified time (one week, three days, two weeks, whatever is decided). It can only be removed if the conditions of an agreement have been met; such as, all chores should be done with a happy attitude, not one gripe will be voiced during the said time, or during the bonus time the chores for each day will be completed *before* 9:00 a.m. Use anything that will bring about an improvement in attitude or application. At the end of the time period, if the agreement has been met, they have "earned" whatever is hidden under the "bonus stamp." This can range from a double-dip ice cream cone to a movie. It should be

31

NAME

	MONDAY	TUESDAY	WEDNESDAY	THURSDAY	FRIDAY	SATURDAY	SUNDAY
EVERY DAY teeth straighten your room make bed get up with a smile help with dishes or vacuum :)							
	Dust & clean living room and dining room	clean own bedroom spic & span also vacuum the floor	FREE DAY	Sweep Kitchen Porch and walks	take out trash and pick up trash from yard	Family Projects & Outings	Heavenly Fathers Day
	Prepare treat and/or games		Activity Night	Primary		Prepare for Sunday	
	FAMILY NIGHT						

(chores assigned according to age)

Holiday Time Chore Charts Can Be Fun!

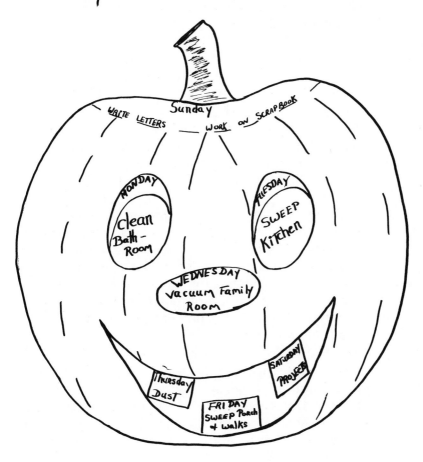

within the range of what was accomplished and their age. Lots of times it can be only for fun, since you don't want to form the habit of having to bribe your family for help. This idea is used maybe two or three times a year at our house. It has become a competitive thing to see if everyone can make it all of the way through to find what is under the "stamp." It is used to break the monotony, but it is not the general rule.

— Use a Box or a Bowl

Another variation of the chore chart can be a box or bowl. Write a chore and a day of the week on a slip of paper. Write an equal amount of chores to be divided among the family. Place all the slips of paper in a box. On family night, have the children "draw straws", each one drawing an equal amount of slips. Slip in several "free days." If one child gets more than one free day or duplicate chores, it is understood he puts them back into the box and draws again. These are the chore assignments for the next week or so. Give each individual a piece of paper to tape or glue his assignments onto. This prevents them from becoming conveniently lost.

— Another idea for a simple chore chart is a family blackboard. This can quickly be written in the morning, or better yet the night before. This way the family can see at a glance what is outlined for the day. Each individual member can check to see what time they are expected to be home to help with some specific task.

Do the Same Thing Differently

Look for ways to transform an ordinary chore into an exciting adventure.

Instead of telling your twelve-year-old daughter to scrub the potatoes and put them in the oven an hour before you come home from work that night, why not send her a post

Saturday's Super-Colossal Bonus Activities

1. Vacuum — very well — living room
   furniture ....10 Large
                                   Bonus Points

2. Clean with dry brush & vacuum —
   then spot with damp cloth —
   dining room furniture ....10 Large
                                   Bonus Points

3. Dust, furniture, vases and things —
   carefully ....8 Large
                                   Bonus Points

4. Clean and straighten bathroom ....8 Large
                                   Bonus Points

5. Vacuum — very well — rugs,
   floor and hall ....8 Large
                                   Bonus Points

6. Straighten kitchen and put away all
   you can ....10 Large
                                   Bonus Points

7. Clean window sills ....2 Large
                                   Bonus Points

8. Mop floors ....6 Large
                                   Bonus Points

Find out what the bonus points are by joining in our "activity"!

card saying the same thing? Allow time for the card to travel through the mail. Be sure to say exactly what day, date and time she is to do her chore.

Saturday morning is a good time for cleaning projects. Don't announce matter-of-factly that everyone will help clean — or else. Try a little pre-planning.

In the middle of the week (so no one will be able to say they didn't know about it), make a grand, enthusiastic announcement: "Everyone is invited to Saturday's Super-Colossal Bonus Activities. Starting time: 9:00 a.m." Then make a poster such as that on the accompanying page.

You decide what the bonus points will equal. You can get a lot done in a short period of time, and your family will have fun doing it.

36

Learning to work together and sharing the responsibilities of certain chores definitely has advantages. It creates a smoother run home, helps you the working mother, and the young people grow as well. This is not inferring that children whose mothers are at home do not learn responsibility; they do. However, children whose mothers work usually feel the weight of the responsibility more.

Sense of Humor

When sharing responsibilities, try to maintain a sense of humor. After working eight hours a day, it is easy to carry home the pressures and tensions of the job. It is not easy, however, for the family to understand why Mom is always in a hurry, always rushing, always pushing. I imagine, in their realm of understanding, it seems rather unreasonable. They can't comprehend that in so many hours a report has to be done and, at the same time, another assignment should have been done twenty minutes ago. So try to rid yourself of the "job atmosphere." You're home now. Yes, things must be done; and no, you haven't any time. But, how many times will your family accept their share of the workload, if you're always saying, "Not now, I don't have time," or "Not now, I'm too tired"?

A sense of humor can help counteract all the tiredness, tension and whatever else you feel as you rush home and try to keep everybody else rushing too. Sometimes, things reach a point where you have to laugh or cry. It becomes a much happier environment if you learn to laugh first.

"Each task can be loosely wrapped with the strings of a sense of humor." This ideal quotation should set the goal for us. Most situations work out better for all concerned if you maintain a sense of humor.

In "The Art of Rearing Children Peacefully," Emma Ray Riggs McKay expresses an attitude that working women (or any mother) would be wise to incorporate in their lives. Many times, schedules are so hurried and time seems so short that you lose patience with your families. Mrs. McKay is referring to husbands in her article, but it can apply to children as well.

37

"Suppose you ask your husband to carry a mattress downstairs. Instead of carrying it carefully so that not a speck of dirt touches its clean coverage, he throws it through the window upon the lawn below. He probably did not think of the grimy dirt from the window frames soiling the cover nor of the possible dirt that might be on the lawn. All he wanted to do was to save time and energy and get the thing over with in a hurry. Will you rant and rave at him, call him a stupid creature who never does things right; or will you think, 'Oh, what's the use? The thing is done. Better make the best of it'? Always the latter if you can make yourself be calm. Even a slightly sarcastic remark will bring a disagreeable answer, and you'll wish you had not said a word."[2]

[2]Emma Ray Riggs McKay, "The Art Of Rearing Children Peacefully" (Extension Publications, Brigham Young University, Provo, Utah, April 12, 1962).

If a child breaks a bowl or glass, it doesn't do any good to fly into a rage. It only causes confusion and hurt feelings and doesn't help one bit. The glass or bowl is already broken. An outburst of unthinking anger will not replace it. How much better, if you help the child clean it up, trying to teach him to be more careful in the future. Express the thought that you are grateful he was not cut seriously. Would the child then know which was more important to Mom, the glass or himself?

When we moved from California to Utah, we left behind our luxurious, automatic dishwasher. Prior to the move, we had so many glasses that they were crowded on several cupboard shelves. Within a few weeks, we began to notice the toll human dishwashers were taking on the glassware.

It became a nightly process to count the remaining glasses, in awe at how fast they were disappearing.

One night as they set the table, my son and daughter started cheering. They had found enough glasses of one style to have a matched set for dinner.

This could have become a problem and a source of contention. Instead, we took enough money from the grocery budget one month to buy sturdy plastic tumblers. Now if we use matching glasses, it is a special occasion. It has become a family joke.

Try to keep a proper balance between what is a catastrophe and what is an occurrence of everyday life. If you become upset over every accident and every problem, your children will be mixed up, not knowing what is truly a serious offense. This does not mean you become apathetic, but you should try to be consistent and just in your discipline. Take advantage of problem situations to provide meaningful teaching moments.

Chapter Four

After-Hours Housework Made Easier

Housework, especially when you work at a full-time job away from home, can become a real drudgery. Cleaning will be the same tomorrow as it is today. You will have to vacuum, dust, and do the dishes — *again*. Some tasks must be repeated over and over — the same as at work. Your attitude will determine whether housework is an unglamorous monotony or a challenge, something to accomplish while you're struggling for a goal.

Getting *all* the housework done after working eight hours is truly a challenge. Planning and scheduling is a "must."

The overall responsibilities and tasks are never quite caught up, never quite finished; but the daily tasks can be accomplished.

This chapter includes encouraging suggestions to help you to get through the housework and chores.

A work plan is a valuable time-saver. Make a list of your duties, and try to keep to a schedule.

Start with a master schedule listing the basic household chores that have to be done daily, weekly, monthly, seasonally, semiannually, or annually.

Next, list those tasks, step by step in logical order, that have to be done through the day. Or, simply list the most important chores that have to be done that day. You feel a growing sense of accomplishment as you cross things off and watch the list shrink. Of course, if one weekly item shows up on a list four weeks in a row, you get the picture — you really don't want to do it.

The working woman often gets so bogged down in repetitious routine that she can't see how to make her tasks easier.

The best rule for easier housecleaning is that familiar "A place for everything and everything in its place." Some suggest putting every out-of-place object in a "junk basket" until the owner misses it enough to claim it. Naturally some items will take up permanent residency in the basket, and eventually you will have to decide what to do with them. But it is one way to keep the house picked up.

40

Don't let your ambition run away with you. You can clean well without wearing yourself to a "frazzle." Do a little at a time.

A little change can do a lot to boost your morale. Arrange some flowers in a vase. (If you can't afford flowers and have none in your yard, try some pretty weeds.) Put out a fancy dish filled with candy. Do something different, if only to change the position of a chair or to switch around the throw rugs.

Can you enjoy housework, especially after a long day on the job? Yes! Make it more pleasant. Turn the radio on to a station that plays your kind of music, or put on a stack of your favorite records. Music will soothe you. Remember to "whistle while you work." I don't recommend that you dance with the broom, but a cheerful atmosphere helps considerably. Sit down whenever the chore allows. A stool with adjustable height helps in many situations.

Pamper yourself. Don't work until you are weary. Short breaks allow you to catch a second wind.

Your work clothes at home are as important as those you wear on the job. Wear comfortable shoes that support your feet. Changing shoes when you arrive home will rest your feet, but sloppy slippers will wear you out even more.

There are many cleaning products on the market. Choose a basic one that works for you, and stick with it. When you're not working, you will have time to read labels and try new remedies.

The best way to clean is not to have to clean. Try a few tricks to save time for other things.

Use door mats so everyone can wipe the dirt off *before* coming in.

Use scatter rugs in heavy traffic areas. They are quick and easy to wash.

Casters under beds and furniture are relatively inexpensive and make cleaning easier and simpler.

Use aluminum foil or cookie sheets under foods in the oven that might run over.

If you don't have an automatic dishwasher, perhaps washing dishes once a day would suffice. If there is adequate storage space, scrape, rinse and stack the morning dishes. In the evening do them all in one fell swoop. This, of course, will not be practical if you have a large family.

Alternate heavy and light jobs.

If possible, work with the windows open. After being closed in all day at work, the fresh air is refreshing.

Explore the stores every once in a while to find time-saving and helpful household gadgets.

41

Learn to use the equipment you already have to its fullest capacity. Do you know the many ways your vacuum cleaner attachments can help to ease the chores? If you have a floor scrubber, do you know how to take advantage of it? Read the manufacturer's directions, keep your appliances in good condition, and then use them.

Don't expend all your energy by mopping floors on your hands and knees. A long-handled mop works as well, and it eliminates sore knees and backache.

Fold sheets, towels, sox, underwear, etc., as they come from the dryer or line. They are fresh and clean, and there is no need to iron them.

Don't underestimate the abilities and will of your children, all ages. Even the very young can help. They can empty waste baskets, vacuum, sweep, dust, polish furniture, help fold clothes, put things away, and pick up toys.

42

Line your shelves and drawers with plastic- or rubber-coated shelf liner, or wash and apply several coats of wax. That way the shelf can just be wiped clean. Do one shelf or drawer at a time. It only takes a minute.

Clean up as you go along to avoid an all-out, clean-everything-at-once project. The house will remain presentable, livable, never really dirty; and it takes less out of you in the long run.

For "quickie" cleanups in the bathroom and kitchen, keep a set of cleansers and sponges in each room.

Teach everyone who is old enough that they wash out the tub and basin after each use.

The little things add up too, like replacing soap and toilet tissue when it is used up.

When it came to the laundry, it seemed I could never keep up with it. It would take ages to sort it. The only place I had to sort was our bedroom, since our house was extremely small. I didn't have time to do a whole wash in one day, so the sorted clothes "graced" our bedroom floor for a day or two each week. And, after stumbling over them several times, I had to sort again. Something had to be done.

My daughter and I went to the produce department of the local grocery store and asked for several apple boxes. At home, we used our faithful felt-tip pens to "design" individual hampers for each bedroom and the bathroom. Now it's much neater and easier to do single batches of laundry. It's faster to sort from smaller sources. The hamper in the bathroom is for "towels only." That load doesn't even have to be sorted, just carried out and put into the washer.

If you have to wash at the local laundromat, save time by sorting your clothes into machine-size batches before you go. Then they can be popped right into the washers. The only problem is remembering how many washers have your clothes in them.

43

Find a fairly large, flat box; fold items directly from the dryer, placing them neatly into the box. Put things away as soon as you get home. Take along an ironing caddy and hangers. Hang up permanent-press items directly from the dryer.

If you find that you still must iron some items, use an adjustable ironing board. Iron while sitting down. Keep an ironing caddy handy to hang up the ironed clothes. This eliminates getting up and down to find a doorway or closet rod. And the ironed clothes can be put away in one trip instead of many.

If things get bogged down and you don't have older children to help you, perhaps one Saturday morning, every other month or so, you could offer to pay one of the neighborhood teen-agers to help. For your morale and the benefit of the help, it could be a worthwhile investment.

The housekeeping tasks need not be restricted to the girls in the family. Boys should also be encouraged to develop these talents. Girls can help with the yard work too.

Simplify your routines. Lay out your clothes the night before, so that you will waste no time deciding what to wear or dressing in the morning. The same applies to your children.

Stop feeling guilty, and try a more relaxed and practical approach. If you feel good and your family feels good about your home, then you are a good housekeeper.

44

Chapter Five

Time a Commodity

One thing all working women have in common is lack of time. Time seems to be the commodity that you have the least of. It would seem that some kind soul would invent a clock with at least twenty-nine hours in every day, just for working women.

Raising a family, making a living, outside responsibilities, church jobs — you have to find time for all of them. To maintain a well-run house you must accomplish a great many tasks, and you have relatively no time to do them.

It may be a surprising fact, but working women spend almost as much time on housework as do women who remain at home.

In a church meeting one evening, a young man was speaking about the importance of making good use of our time, especially the time that is spent with the family. He repeated the often-quoted "It isn't the quantity of time we spend with our families but the quality that makes the difference."

Feeling sorry for myself because I had to work, I sat there making snide comments to myself: "Yes, he could make comments like that. He didn't have to be a mother and work too." About the time my thoughts had really started to churn, my son poked me in the ribs. Grinning from ear to ear he whispered: "We're sure lucky we don't have any of those kind of problems. We have quantities of quality."

I guess you know who went through a quick session of repenting.

All of us know someone who works and manages to get more done in one day than we can accomplish in three days. They seem to have a knack. More than likely it's an ability that has been developed over a period of time. This ability comes from planning ahead and scheduling. The result of doing so is not just more tasks and jobs accomplished but more time found for leisure and enjoyable pastimes.

Whenever anyone mentions doing *more* to a working woman, they are treading on dangerous ground.

46

But, are you sure you're using all of the time you do have? Take a few moments to perform an experiment. Get a fairly large bowl. Fill it with apples or oranges. The bowl is full. Isn't that right? No. Now put some walnuts into the bowl. Is the bowl full now? Pour a handful of beans in between the apples and nuts. Surely the bowl must be full. No, it's not. Add a handful of rice, shaking the bowl a little bit to work in the rice. Now the bowl is *starting* to get full.

Liken the bowl to your day. The priority tasks are the apples and walnuts. Even though your day looks full, there is still room for other things.

This book tries to offer the help needed by a variety of women, with different situations and different points of view. I doubt if there is anyone who can do everything that is suggested. For her to do so, she would require twenty-nine hours a day, and then she would probably be unbearable to live with.

But whether you are rich or poor in hours or dollars, you

can have a full life by your own standards. For some people, this will take much more figuring and philosophy-building than for others.

Develop a philosophy for getting everything done when there is a lot to do. When you work, this is everyday. Organize before you leap. Check things over. Do the easiest first, and then do the next easiest. In this way you get a lot done and out of the way in a hurry.

Learn to set priorities. When you work, you must budget your time. If you don't have a plan, you usually have chaos. This leads to discouragement and depression. It is easy to get bogged down and discouraged.

Your first priority must be *organization*. An encouraging thought is that being organized means different things to different people. You will not all become organized to the same degree. But being organized can be developed just as other talents can. It requires persistence and desire.

47

Climb Out of Your Rut

Do you need to climb out of a rut? Every day you dig your rut deeper. Ruts can be good or bad. Analyze yours. "No rut should be so deep that you can't, from a standing position, jump out of it."[1]

Take a look — a good honest look — at your habits. Sort out your priorities. Throw out those that are no longer meaningful, and adopt a few new ones that will allow you to be happier with your situation. It takes time to incorporate new habits and ideas. However, if they are worthwhile and will improve your situation, work at them.

Worry Is a Villain

Worry tends to be a great time-waster, a robber of peace and contentment, a true villain for stirring up our emo-

[1]Florence B. Pinnock, *Of Food and Thought* (Deseret Book Co., Salt Lake City, Utah, 1965), p. 17.

tions and common sense. As a working woman, your "worry load" can become monstrous, if you allow it to. When you have many problems in varying degrees of importance, it is easy to spend a lot of time dwelling on them. Worrying about or dwelling on a subject with a negative attitude is much different than constructive brainstorming to find a workable solution. Worry slows you down and doesn't bring a solution any nearer. You are using only a portion of your thinking power.

How then can you not worry with so much to accomplish and so little time to do it in?

Hours and days slip by if you have no plan. Get to know yourself better. Realize you are not your neighbor or your best friend, whom you admire a great deal. Know your capabilities, and especially your limitations. Be flexible. Recognize the fact that there will be many days when you just cannot get it all done. Form an attitude that you have the most polite housework and chores of anyone in the neighborhood. They never nag or complain; they sit quietly, waiting until you get around to them. A basket full of ironing or a hamper full of washing does not mean that you are a total failure.

48

Worry — in an excessive amount — will not allow you to win.

The story is told of a man who was burdened with many problems but didn't let them hinder him. He said he did all of his worrying from 6:00 to 6:30 each night; the rest of the time he concentrated on how he was going to accomplish his tasks, without a thought wasted on worries.

Leisure a Necessity

Don't become a martyr! Everyone needs time to relax, especially you who carry on two full-time careers. You are entitled to a day or two, every now and then, when you are totally "good for nothing" — except sitting with your feet up and being waited on (if you can get away with it).

Leisure is not a luxury, it is a necessity. You need time to sit back and daydream about your castles in the air, to think about the superb project that you are about to embark upon. Leisure periods can be rewarding and productive. When you work, work. When you relax, do something you enjoy, such as reading a chapter in a good book, taking a walk, or saying hello to your neighbor. Give yourself twenty minutes. Then go back with renewed energy to tackle the mountain of chores.

Plan Ahead to Get Ahead

Planning ahead is most helpful in getting things done and allowing you to make the most of the time you have. Here are tips and ideas to help you make the most of that time:

Plan tomorrow today; when tomorrow comes, you won't have to waste time planning. Each evening reserve five to ten minutes to plan tomorrow. A good time to think about what needs to be scheduled might be as you prepare the evening meal. Put a note pad on a free corner of your sink and jot down items as you think of them. Later, take a few minutes to check the calendar and organize the list in order of priorities.

49

We have already discussed chore charts for the children. A chore chart for mother is not such a bad idea either. If you have a small project to do every evening, just one chore, it will save some of that precious time on Saturday to spend at leisure or with the family. Pick up and clean one room a night. Put in a batch of laundry one night, then vacuum or straighten the living room the next.

The last time I made my children's chore charts, I made one for myself too. It gave me a sense of accomplishment. When Saturday morning came, the laundry was done and the house almost looked presentable. It became a personal challenge each evening to catch a second wind and then keep going until I had at least one thing done.

Remember, lists and schedules are only supposed to be

helpful guides. Remain flexible. Don't let your schedule become a slave driver. No matter what kind of nutritious meal you have planned, if the opportunity comes to eat out, do so.

Take one day at a time. Do your best. As long as you try, there is no need for a guilt complex.

Try not to compare your accomplishments with your neighbor who does not have to work at a full-time job away from the home. You and she operate in completely different circles, even though in many areas the circles are the same.

I have found a large wall calendar is a great help. You can make or buy one. Make sure it has large spaces to write in. Things to do, appointments, reminders, special days, etc., can all be seen at a glance. Your calendar can even be color coded. Use crayon pencils or different shades of ink: anything in red is an absolute must; green indicates it would be nice if there is time; a birthday in purple.

50

Group Your Tasks

Group tasks to save time. This can be done in almost any area, if you think about it.

Hold your correspondence until you can answer several letters at once. Combine paying the bills and writing a few short notes. Time is precious, but so are relatives and friends. Note stationery, fold-over notes, or even colorful post cards can carry short messages until you have a spare day to write nice long letters.

If you have to go to the garage or basement for one item, check to see what other items need to be brought back at the same time. Save yourself another trip later.

Try to do all of the errand running once a week or every other week, instead of going out every time you think of something. Continual running cuts deeply into the few evening hours at home.

Plan an hour one evening a week to make all your business phone calls. Take a few minutes to jot down the necessary things to be said. This will save time in getting to the point. Talk no longer than necessary.

Collect your mending in one box or basket. One evening, when there is an especially interesting program on television, sew on buttons or darn a few socks.

Minute Projects

"You would be wise to have some minute projects or even some second projects. Sew on a button while you talk on the phone, pick up as you walk through your home or yard, paste in trading stamps while the vegetables are boiling, or tuck a paper in the file each time you walk past."[2] These minutes quickly add up; and you'll have accomplished a great deal.

Break larger chores into several small projects. For example: clean the sink in the bathroom while you're waiting for your child's tub to fill. Disinfect the toilet bowl while you're bathing, insuring that no child gets into it.

51

Set some long-range goals that you can pick up and work on a few minutes at a time. This book has been written in fifteen-minute spurts, with an occasional hour-long session. In our living room hangs a picture of the Last Supper which is done in cross-stitch embroidery. This beautiful piece of artwork took my mother-in-law four years to complete, a stitch at a time, while she was working full-time.

Remember the bowl of apples and walnuts? Your day's bowl of time still has room for "minute rice."

Rise Early (Earlier)

Getting up is the hardest chore of the day for me. Yet when I make the supreme effort of getting up even one-

[2]Daryl Hoole, *The Art of Homemaking* (Deseret Book Co., Salt Lake City, Utah, 1963), p. 51.

half hour earlier so that I'm not rushed, it never ceases to amaze me how much smoother the day seems to go.

One woman shared some thoughts on the benefits of rising early. She reported: "This year I've tried to get to bed at a decent hour and arise at 5:00 a.m. for three hours of concentrated effort before I prepare to leave home. I've divided this time into half-hour intervals: exercising; sewing; playing the piano; preparing an attractive breakfast; doing dishes; making beds and picking up; then, if there's time, back to sewing, writing a letter or whatever needs topping off. By doing this, much is accomplished before I have to leave for work."

My mother-in-law has worked as long as I have known her. She has raised six children. It has always been her habit to arise between 4:00 and 5:00 a.m. to do the housework. I've often asked her, "Mom, how can you do it?" Since returning to work, I appreciate her attitude: "I can always get more done, much quicker, when the children aren't around. I'd rather do it early, than to have to come home tired, after working all day, and put in the same amount of hours. I have more ambition when it is early."

52

One help to start the day, especially if you have a large family, is to set the table for breakfast the night before. The first time I tried doing this, my husband came home from a meeting about 8:30 p.m. He took his books and jacket into the bedroom. I listened as he went into the kitchen and opened the refrigerator door, then the oven door. He then stood in the doorway with a sheepish look on his face and said: "I can't remember, have we eaten supper or haven't we? And if we haven't, what are we going to eat? There's nothing ready, and it's not very early."

"Hurry" Is a Villain

I have discovered that "hurry" can be as big a villain as worry. Somehow the word crept into my vocabulary so frequently that it soon lost its meaning. I became so bogged down with the multitude of things that had to be done that everything was hurried.

Perhaps this is another area where you need to be corrected, as I did.

Force yourself to consider the other members of the family. Surely every time you go to the store you don't have to "hurry." When you enter the store, calmly say, "Tonight we need to be finished with our shopping in thirty minutes," or whatever time should be allowed.

Getting ready for bed would be happier and more peaceful for everyone concerned if a "pajama time" was established. Then there could be a time for talk, stories or ten more minutes of television, instead of "hurry," tears and short tempers.

Maybe the dishes could be a race against the timer or someone doing another chore, rather than "hurry and get through."

53

Once in a while, when time is truly short, ask your son or daughter or husband to do something "super fast."

"Hurry" needs to be put into proper perspective and not misused.

Think of how you react on the job if for three days in a row every single task is labeled Expedite, Rush, Top Priority, or Due Twenty Minutes Ago. It doesn't take long for you to become "frazzled," keyed up, and totally unhappy with the situation. Your family reacts in the same way.

From now on, resolve that "hurry" will cease to exist, except for the occasion when it will really mean something.

Busy People Accomplish

You may not be able to spend twenty-four hours at home; but if you make wise use of the minutes, bit by bit, you *can* accomplish a great deal. The old saying holds true. "If you want to get something done, ask a busy person to do it." Those who are busy and have limited time aren't usually prone to waste it.

There is no substitute for wife or mother. You must learn how to save time in other areas — such as in your house-work — in order to have time for your family. The well-run home is not run with a clock; it is run with the heart. Time-saving can prove to be life-saving.

54

Chapter Six

What to Do About Baby-Sitters

The lives of our children should be our first concern, far ahead of anything else on our list of priorities. The best of all situations is being able to stay at home and care for them. The necessity to work creates difficulties. Having to leave your child in the daily care of another individual is extremely difficult. The child must be left when cute and cuddly, whether sick or well, when having personal problems, with the first tooth coming through, and so on. All this causes emotional turmoil within mothers. It is hard to accept the fact that someone else will, for all intents and purposes, be raising your child most of the time. It therefore becomes imperative to make proper decisions about the care of your child while you must work.

For a baby or a small child, you'll need to find a baby-sitter. For a child of three or older, you might consider a nursery school or day care center.

The decision as to who will care for your child and how is a complex problem. There are many influencing factors: your budget, the ages and number of your children, how far you must travel to work, and more.

Here are some ideas and suggestions to help you make that decision.

Choosing a Baby-Sitter

If at all possible have a relative or close friend — someone you know well and trust — care for your child.

If that is not possible, be extremely selective. Take the time to find the "right" sitter. Look for someone who can give something special, so that the child will benefit from having had an association with her.

Unless the sitter is a personal friend or relative, it is a good idea to choose a licensed sitter. A license guarantees periodic checks by the Department of Health and the Fire Department. There are usually strict requirements as to how many children can be cared for in one household, not allowing overcrowding of the facilities in order to have more income. A license also ensures a standard of cleanliness. (But, remember, there is a difference between being dirty and having "lived-in clutter.")

56

Do not be afraid to ask for personal references from anyone you would consider as a baby-sitter. These could come from previous employers or reliable people. When you apply for employment, you will be asked for references; you should require no less from someone who will have the responsibility of your child.

Try to find a warm, understanding person who will have patience and accept your child as an individual. Have standards and expectations for your sitter.

Does the sitter's definition of discipline agree with yours in all areas? What kind of discipline and how severe a punishment is acceptable? Do you want your child to be spanked under any circumstances? What kind of restrictions are acceptable? Strict guidelines need to be set that are agreeable to everyone concerned.

If your child is old enough, take him to visit the sitter before you make a decision. Be observant. Does the individual care enough to try to establish a relationship with your child? Does she speak kindly and with the kind of language you want your child to pick up? Does she smile quickly and easily?

How many children are in her care during the day? Is she more profit-conscious than child-conscious? Can she give the proper amount of time and care to your child?

All kinds of tales are told about the horrors of baby-sitters and the unhappy situations children are placed in. This is not always the case. Many women are kind and loving. There was a time when I baby-sat other children. One little girl and her brother became "mine." I cared for them for several years. I learned to love them dearly and treated them in the same manner as my own children. I have seen many such situations, where love and proper care are given. There are probably as many "case histories" *for* as against baby-sitters.

57

Take precautions, be very selective, and you probably will not have any problems. However, do not hesitate one minute to remove your child from the home of someone whose care is inferior, or that might be harmful.

Taking your child to a baby-sitter may offer him more comfortable security than a nursery school or day care center would.

You also need to consider the pros and cons of having someone come into your home to baby-sit as opposed to taking your child into another person's home.

There are several advantages to having your child remain in your own home. Probably the most obvious one, you wouldn't have to take him out in case of illness. The child would remain in a familiar environment for naps and playmates. Toys and play equipment would be familiar also. Usually you would be aware of the menus and foods being prepared.

On the other hand, for your situation, it might work out better to take your child to a sitter's home. Perhaps the sitter has some children of her own who would provide worthwhile companionship and learning experiences.

Important Information for the Sitter

There are several items of information that you need to provide and keep current for your sitter.

A signed permission slip is an absolute necessity so that your child can receive proper medical attention in case of an emergency or illness. Check with your doctor's office to see if a specific form or other requirement is necessary for someone other than the parent to bring a child in for treatment.

Your sitter needs a list of phone numbers where you can be reached in case of an emergency. You need to discuss specifically what measures should be taken, priorities, and if there is someone to contact in case you cannot be reached immediately. These instructions should be written down.

If your child requires medication this should be strictly outlined — what can or cannot be given and when. You need to establish whether or not you want medicines, such as aspirin, given if the child becomes ill during the day. Do not take this kind of care for granted. *Be specific.*

Have an Available Alternate

Remember, your sitter is a person with needs and problems. There may be days when she becomes ill or has her own emergency. You should have a friend or neighbor, with whom you have made prior arrangements, that you can call on the spur of the moment to help you out. Make arrangements with your sitter to contact you by a certain time, so that you won't be late or miss work because of a last-minute scramble.

58

The Day Care Center

Another possibility or alternative you might want to consider is a day care center.

In most areas there is a difference between nursery schools and day care centers. However, the name varies from state to state and area to area, the greatest difference being the length of time your child is expected to remain in attendance. Preschool and nursery schools are usually for a few hours in the morning or afternoon for children three to five years old. A program is usually taught in crafts, ABC's and social development. The mothers of these children generally do not work away from the home. A light snack is usually served.

A day care center provides regular all-day care for children while parents must work. They generally are geared to offer more than regular baby-sitter services. Scheduled programs are offered for the development of the children. Warm, nutritionally balanced lunches are served, as well as morning and afternoon snacks.

59

Your child has a chance to mix with other children of the same age. An organized program of development, learning and social adjustment can be beneficial.

Cost is a large factor in deciding whether to take your child to a day care center. In any case, a day care center is not recommended for a child under three years old.

Requirements for a Good Day Care Center

— A loving and accepting teacher, who loves children and who has a warm personality.
— A program which will increase the child's capacity and abilities, and give him a firm academic foundation.
— Clean, bright, friendly facilities in a good location for you.

—Wholesome, nutritious food, prepared in clean sur-
roundings.

It is important to take the time to observe the environment
you are considering for your child. Here are a few things to
look for. Some of them were mentioned earlier in connec-
tion with the quest for a private baby-sitter.

—Are the children happy and interested? Look at their
eyes and look for smiles.
—Is there a good interrelationship with the teacher?
—Does the teacher smile and put her arms around the
children once in a while? Is her care and concern for
the children visible?
—Does the teacher speak in a warm, kind voice?
—Is the artwork of the children abundantly displayed?
—Are the toys child-oriented?
—Does the center offer a mediumly structured program, where the child is allowed freedom to explore,
grow and develop? Are there defined behavior roles
with other children?
—Is the director warm and friendly?
—Taking your child with you will give you an idea as to
how the director appeals to your child and vice versa.
Does the director care enough to try to establish a
relationship with your child, or is her main concern
getting the child for monetary reasons?

You need to ask several questions, especially if you have
not had any previous contact with a day care center. Be
sure to ask lots of questions *before* placing your child in a
particular center. You need to know:

—How are the children grouped?
—What teacher will your child have? Is he or she steady,
full-time, part-time or volunteer?
—How many different teachers will your child have?
—What type of program is offered? What kind of
academics are offered?

— What kind of schedule — the ratio of teacher-guided time to play time?

— What kind of "pacing" of the children is used in their schedule?

— How long a period of time is required to be spent on a certain subject (twenty minutes, thirty minutes, an hour)?

— What toys are available? Are they educational as well as play toys?

— What is the teacher-pupil ratio? Is it according to code?

— What are the backgrounds of the teachers? Their qualifications?

— Are there facilities for outside play and physical exercise?

— How many television sets are there and how much time is spent watching them? How are the programs selected?

— How long has the school been under the current management?

61

If you are new to an area and would like references for a day care center, contact the neighborhood schools or the county or church social service offices.

Keep Home a Haven

Remember to have a listening ear when your child comes home from the baby-sitter's or the day care center. If he is old enough to talk, this important time of sharing will tell you much about the care he is receiving. If you listen, you can pick up the thread of the day and wrap the child close to you with security and love.

No matter how careful you are, there will still be problems — more so than if you could be at home without the pressures of working. Try to solve the problems as easily and peacefully as possible. Keep home a secure haven to return to at the end of each day.

Chapter Seven

Meals and Menus

As a working woman, one of the most difficult challenges you have is to feed yourself and your family properly and pleasantly in a very limited amount of time (usually with a limited amount of energy).

This is one area that needs thought and planning. You do not have the time to prepare elaborate or involved meals. When you work, you tend to gravitate towards the "convenience" foods because they are supposedly the quickest and easiest. This trend, however, causes your food budget to rise drastically.

As you plan meals, don't forget the nutritional value in foods. The importance of good food in our lives cannot be understated. The way you eat determines your health and energy. It also teaches children eating habits that will continue throughout their lives.

"Above all, eating is and should be fun . . . a time to bring the family together around the table; a time to stop and reflect on the rich harvest. . . . Breakfast can be a time of sharing the hope for a bright and happy day; dinner the occasion of telling the tales of an eventful day. Mealtime can always be a time of sharing, whether it is at a dinner table, barbeque or picnic. The focus on food can mean fun, friendship and good health."[1]

Stick to simple, wholesome meals, and save the gourmet dinners for weekends and holidays.

Choose foods from the basic four food groups to supply a normal healthy individual with most of the recommended daily allowances of essential nutrients.

What foods should you choose? The key word is "variety." Prepare meals using foods from all four groups, and your diet will include the proper nutrients.

BASIC FOUR FOOD GROUPS

1. Meat Group . . .
   2 or more servings daily. Includes meat, fish, poultry and eggs. Alternate beans, peas, lentils and nuts. Good sources of protein

63

2. Dairy Foods . . .
   2 cups daily for adults
   3-4 cups daily for children
   4 cups or more daily for teen-agers, pregnant women
   This group includes milk, cheeses, ice cream, dairy products. Good sources of vitamin A, protein and riboflavin

3. Fruit and Vegetable Group . . .
   4 or more servings daily
   1 serving green or yellow vegetable
   1 serving citrus fruit or tomato (or source of vitamin C)
   2 or more servings of other fruits and vegetables
   Good sources for vitamins A and C

4. Bread and Cereal Group . . .
   4 or more servings daily
   Includes all breads and cereal grains

[1]Metropolitan Life Insurance Co., *New Metropolitan Cook Book* (Metropolitan Life Insurance Co., New York, N.Y.), p. 1.

Good sources for B vitamins, iron, some protein, carbohydrates

This chapter will help you find quick and easy ways to prepare well-balanced meals in limited time.

I was trying to be a good mother and feed my family properly, taking care to serve a well-balanced, nutritious breakfast to provide a good start for each day. I had explained to the family how important nutrition and vitamins are and why it is so important for us to eat good foods.

I purchased a cereal that we had not had before, because it had lots of iron in it. About a week later at the supper table, I brought up the nutrition subject again and asked if the family liked the new cereal. My son and daughter looked at each other and burst out laughing.

64

Erin explained that he had been thoroughly enjoying the cereal. In fact he was eating his second bowlful one morning while reading the box about all of the good things the cereal had in it, "just like Mom said it did." Then he could eat no more, for there in print it said "gentle laxative." "I worried for two days at school that I was going to have problems and have to be excused from class all day long."

Oh, well! There went all of my good plans.

Marketing

Before you are able to prepare meals, you must go shopping. On a working woman's schedule, this must be squeezed in somewhere between the laundry and running those other errands.

It can be a harassing, confused, irritating experience. On the other hand, you can make it an enjoyable activity.

If you are married, and have a family, it could be a night out for Mom and Dad. Take care of the shopping necessities, and then have an ice cream cone.

Plan ahead. A little forethought will pay off in the time and effort you save.

Try to arrange shopping trips so that you only have to go to the store every two weeks or, better yet, once a month. (An incredible amount of time would be lost if you had to go to the grocery store every night before preparing a meal.) For in-between shopping trips — for milk, bread or some other small item — buy only what you went for. Don't waste time by browsing. If your children are old enough, send them to the store; or ask your husband to stop on his way home. By spreading out your shopping days, you can cut down on the number of Saturday mornings or Friday evenings you spend in the store, saving this time for other projects.

Never shop without a list. Forgetting to pick up something you needed means another trip. A shopping list also helps you to avoid the impulse buying which leads to higher grocery bills.

Keep a shopping list on the refrigerator, cupboard, or some other obvious, convenient place. Every time you notice an item getting low, or remember one that is needed, write it down. This will not only save time when you shop, but it will eliminate many additional trips because you had forgotten an important ingredient.

65

Divide your shopping list into categories. It will be easier to keep track of things, but the greatest help will be with the actual shopping. An organized list will save minutes (eventually hours) wasted going back and forth between aisles to pick up items listed in a helter skelter manner.

SHOPPING LIST CATEGORIES

Meats	Dairy Products	Produce	Baking Supplies
hot dogs	sour cream	cauliflower	flour
bacon	lge. cottage		soda
chicken	cheese		shortening
	2 doz. eggs		

Juices	Frozen Foods	Canned Goods	Cleansers & Soaps
tomato apple		tuna pork & beans	bleach

Paper Products	Hygiene- Cosmetics	Misc.	Other Errands
T.P. paper towels	deodorant razor blades	dog food new can opener light bulbs vitamins	Cleaners — coat Pick up pattern tire patch birthday card — mail it Post Office — stamps

66

Menu Planning

Plan meals on a daily, weekly or monthly basis, whichever is more convenient for you. Make your menus from your shopping list or vice versa.

We occasionally plan our menus when the whole family is riding to and from meetings or other activities. Everyone contributes suggestions. It saves time, helps me think, and it's fun too.

If you ride the bus or in a car pool, use that time to plan your menus. Once in awhile take a cookbook with you to help stimulate your thinking. On your menu list, jot down the page number of the recipe you want to use.

It might be fun, as well as helpful, to get together with a few co-workers during an occasional lunch hour to swap ideas, hints, and recipes.

If you have trouble with menus and lists, you might want to use a notebook where you can keep track of them. This also makes a good reference book. Look over previous menus for inspiration.

When you try a new recipe, jot the name of the book and page number on your menu sheet. If the recipe is a success it can be transferred to your permanent collection, because you will be able to remember where you found it.

The Right Tools

The best short cuts and time-savers in the kitchen come from having the right equipment. Your tools can be simple and necessary, such as a set of knives. However, they need to be kept in condition, so that knives cut rather than saw.

Take advantage of your mixers, blenders, pressure cookers, electric skillets, and crock pots. If you have forgotten the many jobs each appliance can do, "dig out" the handbook and reread it. These appliances, when used to their full capacity, can save you hours of time in meal preparation. And they make the task much easier.

67

Don't overlook the simple "gadgets" which can streamline your work. Take a browsing trip through a housewares department to see if there might be one or two that could help you.

Clean-up Time

Cleanups should not be left until the end of the meal. *Clean up as you go along.* Wipe up spills immediately, so that you don't have to scrub later.

Dishes can be rinsed out and placed in the dishwasher as they are used to prepare the meal. If you wash by hand, keep the dishpan full of hot, sudsy water. Wash and rinse the dishes and utensils as they are used, and place them in the drainer.

You may not always succeed at this, but when you do the mental boost is tremendous. It leaves only a few dishes to be washed after the meal.

Try a few of these ideas to save yourself work:
— Use aluminum foil or cookie sheets under food in the oven that might spill or run over.
— Cover fry pans or skillets to prevent grease from spattering. If you do not have a lid, use a metal or foil pie pan.
— If you grease more muffin cups than you need, fill the empty ones with water to keep the grease from burning.
— Use a rubber spatula or paper towel to scrape soiled dishes.
— Soak pots and pans in sudsy water as soon as possible.
— Stack like things together, such as silverware, plates, glassware.
— Be sure to allow expansion room in saucepans when cooking things like beans, rice, macaroni, and spaghetti. They boil up quickly and are likely to overflow.

68

Children Can Help

As your children become old enough, teach them to work with you in the kitchen. It's amazing how much fun you can have with them. It will also give you the opportunity for teaching moments on subjects other than cooking. They can learn the sense of accomplishment and satisfaction, especially if you let them know how valuable their help really is. Let them know how much you appreciate a helper at the end of a long workday.

In the morning, or the evening before, prepare a note telling each child what he can do to help get ready for the evening meal. If the children are old enough, the jobs could be done before you arrive home. If they are younger, they can still help.

Children can:
— peel and slice potatoes
— put vegetables in a pan

— make Jello
— fix a salad
— set the table
— cut some flowers (weeds) for the table
— mix the salad dressing
— put such things as salt and pepper, butter, and catsup, on the table
— make biscuits (especially from a mix)
— get out the serving bowls and big spoons
— make celery or carrot sticks
— put ice cubes in glasses
— slice the bread
— put on the napkins
— rinse out the bowls and pans used for food preparation
— help with cleanup and dishes

Children will either get in the way or help, depending on your attitude.

69

A Gourmet Cook?

Have you discovered whether or not your husband is a gourmet cook? Any husband who can open a can of soup and warm it should be considered a gourmet cook by a working wife.

My husband is an excellent cook. This talent runs in his family. His father and all four of his brothers are good cooks. Since I have known his family, Dad has cooked as much or more than Mom because she works too. I'm grateful that this ability and attitude was instilled in my husband, because he does a great deal of the cooking. This in no way depreciates his masculinity; it makes me admire and appreciate him all the more for his willingness to help us work together towards a goal.

However, if husbands can't cook, we don't love them any less. I remember that, as a child, when my mother would get sick, we always knew exactly what the menu would be:

Scrambled eggs and burnt toast! We had to eat the toast, too. My Dad always said, "Some carbon is good for you."

A Few Hints

One or more of the following ideas might fit your situation and help you to prepare your meals.

Don't just open a can of beans; take two extra minutes to do something special so they taste homemade. To a No. 2½ can of pork and beans, add ½ teaspoon of prepared mustard and ¾ cup brown sugar. Mix thoroughly and place in a baking dish. Dot with butter or margarine. Bake at 350°F about 20 minutes while you finish setting the table. Substitute catsup for the mustard as a taste change.

To a package of frozen peas (or canned or fresh), add a small can of mushroom pieces to liven up the everyday meal fare in the middle of the week. (Whole mushrooms make a pretty vegetable dish for a fancy table.)

70

Use "planned overs" to have a quick meal. Try a "smorgasbord" meal, with a little bit of everything. This saves preparation time and prevents wasting food.

Use leftover vegetables in a soup or stew, with leftover gravy as a base.

When the mood comes and you feel like baking, make a triple batch of cookies. Bake some and freeze some. Roll the dough into a sausage shape, five to six inches long by two inches in diameter. Wrap properly so it will not freezer-burn. Put into the freezer. At a later date, when your time is limited and you'd like some fresh cookies, just thaw, slice, and bake.

Breakfast

A good breakfast is the foundation for a happy day. Even if you have to get up fifteen minutes earlier to prepare it. A well-balanced breakfast should make up one-fourth to one-third of the day's total food requirements. A good meal in the morning makes us work better, play better, and feel better all day long.

A good breakfast does not necessarily mean a lumberjack's meal with seven courses. It can be good and quick to prepare.

Perhaps one of the most important aspects of breakfast is that it gives your family a chance to be together, even if it is rushed and only for a few minutes.

There are special touches you can add which will create a happy feeling.

Breakfasts can be varied, by alternating
— the type of main dish served
— the fruits, breads, and beverages served
— the kinds of cereal served
— the ways eggs are cooked
— the kinds of meat served

71

If it is kept simple, the whole breakfast can be changed by substituting even one item.

It has been said that variety is the spice of life; variety also provides spice in breakfasts. Try some of these ideas to perk up your breakfast menus.

Make toast from different kinds of breads. Or serve the many kinds of muffins or biscuits which need only to be heated or made from a mix.

On Saturday morning, make a double batch of waffles. Cook all of them, and freeze the extras. Later in the week, they can be heated in the toaster or oven.

Mix up waffle or pancake batter the night before. Refrigerate in a covered jar. It is ready in the morning for a quick, filling breakfast.

Use leftover fruit — peaches, pears, bananas, fruit cocktail — in a breakfast salad.

Add raisins to applesauce. Serve it warm with cinnamon toast.

Prepare a delicious, quick breakfast cereal with rolled oats, dried or dehydrated apples, and cinnamon. Place ½ to ¾ cups dried apples in water, measured for the amount of cereal you plan to cook. Bring the water to a boil; add ½ teaspoon salt, the oats, and 1 teaspoon cinnamon. Cook to desired thickness. Serve with cream or milk.

To save dishes, mix waffle or pancake batter in a large, wide-mouthed pitcher or the blender. It is then ready to pour onto the griddle.

If breakfast is really rushed one morning, try an eggnog. It is fast and very good for you.

In the blender combine:
   4 cups milk
   2 or 3 eggs
   1 teaspoon vanilla
   2 to 3 teaspoons sugar
   ½ teaspoon nutmeg or cinnamon (optional)

(To make it very rich, add some vanilla ice cream.)

With a slice of bread, this provides a good breakfast.

For an occasional tasty treat, pour melted vanilla ice cream over your cereal, dry or cooked. It creates a happy atmosphere to have a treat early in the morning.

For variety in cooked cereals, add one or a combination of the following:
   — ½ cup dried or dehydrated peaches
   — ½ cup diced dates
   — ¼ cup dehydrated banana flakes
   — ½ cup chopped, dried or dehydrated apples
   — ½ teaspoon cinnamon
   — ½ teaspoon nutmeg
   — ¼ to ½ cup brown sugar

— ¼ cup honey
— ½ cup raisins
— ¼ to ½ cup crushed pineapple with the juice
— ¼ to ½ cup of any of your favorite fruits

MENU IDEAS FOR EASY BREAKFASTS

Fruits	Juices	Main Items	Breads
citrus	tomato	waffles or	toast
oranges	orange	pancakes	muffins
grapefruit	apple	(plain,	(homemade,
bananas	grapefruit	flavored or	mix, or
raisins	pineapple	with fruit	bakery)
berries	grape	added)	quick breads
peaches	cranberry	quick breads	coffee cakes
pears	nectars	(homemade,	doughnuts
melons	prune	mixes, or	yeast rolls
apples		bakery)	
apricots		eggs	
cherries		(vary style)	
fruit salads		cereals	
fruit cocktail		cooked	
(canned,		or dry	
bottled,		french toast	
frozen, in-		eggnog	
season)		meats	
		ham	
		bacon	
		sausage	
		minute steak	
		Canadian	
		bacon	

73

Lunch

Lunch box meals can be dull and unappetizing or they can be attractive and taste good. Opening a lunch box should be something to look forward to. Granted, you can't prepare gourmet lunches every day, but maybe some of these ideas will make packing lunches a little bit easier.

Set aside a regular time, either in the evening or in the morning, to pack lunches. You will be more likely to pack nutritious, balanced lunches if you're not "hurried" into a "last-minute, throw-together" production.

If you have a freezer, a week's supply of sandwiches can be made at one time. Wrap in waxed paper or freezer wrap, labeling each kind of sandwich. Fillings can be made from just about anything: leftover meats ground up with pickles, tuna, salmon, egg salads, a variety of cheeses. Leave mayonnaise, lettuce and tomato out of the sandwiches; add them when you take sandwiches from the freezer. If the sandwich is taken from the freezer at breakfast time, it will be thawed by lunch time. To avoid soggy sandwiches, before freezing them spread softened margarine or butter evenly to the edge of the bread slices.

74

For a nice change, make sandwiches of date nut or banana bread spread with cream cheese. Some fresh carrot or celery sticks and a fresh fruit complete the lunch.

Keep one drawer, or part of one cupboard shelf, for all of your lunch-packing supplies. If you use a cupboard shelf, spare bread pans provide small, stackable drawers to keep things organized. Empty shoe boxes work as well.

Keep a variety of supplies on hand. Some you may find helpful are:
— Small jars (½ pint) with wide-mouth tops and screw lids
— String, tape, rubber bands
— Plastic or wooden forks and spoons
— Small plastic containers, with tight-fitting lids
— Plastic wraps, waxed paper, aluminum foil, and sandwich bags
— Paper napkins
— Salt and pepper shakers

Use vacuum or thermos bottles for warm soups and stews and for cold milk, juices, malts, or milk shakes. Use the smaller wide-mouthed variety for spaghetti, casseroles, chili, beans, macaroni, fruits or vegetables, and salads.

If dinner meals are planned properly, you will have left-overs for nourishing lunches.

Use small glass jars or plastic containers for puddings, gelatin desserts, fruits, and salads — macaroni, tuna, potato, green salads (pack the dressing separately).

Use sandwich bags for crackers, pickles, cucumber or green pepper slices, carrots or celery sticks, lettuce or cabbage wedges, cauliflower florets, cookies, potato chips, nuts, and candies.

Small cans of juice or soft drinks can be frozen and packed with the lunch. This helps to prevent the other foods from spoiling.

75

For a nourishing as well as appetizing lunch, include the following:
  — A protein such as meat, fish, poultry, cheese, eggs or peanut butter.
  — A crisp, crunchy food such as carrot and celery sticks, radishes, pickles, or a salad.
  — A beverage, hot or cold. This could be either a drink or soup.
  — A sweet such as fruit, cookies, or cake.

Evening Meal

The working woman generally finds the evening meal is the hardest to prepare. Usually, you are too tired to consider anything but the fastest and the easiest way to get a meal on the table. Certainly no fancy seven-course meals on Monday nights!

These suggestions may help you prepare good meals in a short time and maybe even give you some fresh ideas on serving some of the old standbys.

Don't worry about serving a hearty meal every evening. Good food value is the key. On days that have been especially trying, serve one of the following:
— Soup and sandwiches
— Waffles, french toast, or pancakes
— Quick hot biscuits and a bowl of fruit and milk
— Bacon, eggs, and hash browns
— Smorgasbord (At our house, this includes the left-overs we can find, served with a new vegetable or two and crackers or bread. Sometimes two pitchers of different kinds of punch make it fun.)
— Rice or bread pudding
— Frozen meat pies and a salad

If you arrive home too tired to cook a complete meal, have a picnic supper. Prepare some sandwiches, spread a blanket on the floor, and use paper plates and paper cups. Have ice cream and cookies for dessert. It can be a fun break for the whole family.

76

Serve vegetables in a quick cream sauce for a change.

MEDIUM CREAM SAUCE

2-3 tablespoons margarine
2-3 tablespoons flour (or corn starch)
¼ teaspoon salt
1 cup milk

Melt margarine in saucepan; add flour and salt. Blend until smooth. Bring to a boil, stirring frequently. Remove from heat and gradually add milk. Cook over low heat until thick. For more quick variety in vegetables, add one or more of the following:
— 1-2 tablespoons bacon crisps
  (Textured Vegetable Protein — TVP)
— 1 tablespoon chopped onion
— 1 tablespoon chopped pimento
— ¼-½ cup mushroom pieces
— 1-2 tablespoons chopped celery

— ¼ to ½ cup bean sprouts
— ¼ to ½ cup alfalfa sprouts
— 1 teaspoon celery seed
— ¼ cup slivered nuts
— 2 tablespoons chopped parsley (or celery leaves)
— 1 hard-boiled egg, chopped

For variety in green salads, add one or more of the following:
— 1-2 tablespoons bacon crisps (TVP)
— 2 teaspoons dill seed
— 1-2 teaspoons celery seed (especially good in cole slaw)
— ¼ to ½ cup sliced mushrooms
— ½ cup raisins
— ½ to ¾ cup croutons or buttered toast, cubed
— ¼ cup chopped nuts
— ½ cup bean sprouts
— ¼ to ½ cup alfalfa, wheat, triticale, or other small seed sprouts
— ½ cup well-drained, canned, diced beets
— ½ cup well-drained, crushed or cubed pineapple
— ½ cup shredded or diced apple
— 2 tablespoons chopped parsley
— 1 hard-boiled egg, chopped
— 1 can luncheon meat, diced
— ½ pound cheddar or mild cheese, diced
— 1 small can cleaned shrimp
— ¼ to ½ cup sliced or chopped olives
— raw cauliflower or broccoli florets

77

You can see how easily you could turn a salad into a complete, wholesome meal.

Use leftover fruits in gelatin. Combine them with small curd cottage cheese and chopped nuts. Gelatin salads are a boon to the working woman because they can be made well ahead of time and in large enough batches to stretch through several meals.

A large batch of potato or macaroni salad can round out several meals. Potato salad can be eaten hot or cold, in the summer or winter.

One-Dish Meals

Skillet dishes or casseroles are time-savers, since they can easily be prepared ahead of time. They are often referred to as dinner-in-a-dish. The ease of "double batching" comes naturally when mixing the ingredients for one-dish meals. The second batch can be frozen and used another day. The saving in cooking and clean-up time is a real bonus. Most of these meals are made by combining all the ingredients in a baking dish or skillet, eliminating many mixing bowls.

78

One-dish meals are adaptable, and the possible variations are almost boundless. There is scarcely a food that cannot be cooked by these methods. It can be simple or elaborate and can fit into almost any meal. Use what you have on hand to create economical dishes. The basic ingredients for making one-dish meals are meat, a combination of meat and vegetables, vegetables, beans, grains, or pastas. While you don't always follow an exact recipe for casseroles or skillet dishes, there are a few general rules.

— Don't use too many ingredients. There should be one main food.
— Use chunks of meat or vegetables for texture. Add eye appeal with bright colors: tomato sauce; chopped, sliced or grated carrots; or sliced olives, pimento, green peppers.
— Build your dishes by giving thought to nutrition, seasoning, and proportion.
— Cook slowly. Casseroles bake, skillet dishes simmer. The flavor develops during the cooking process.

Beans, noodles, macaroni, spaghetti, and rice need to be cooked before adding them to a casserole or skillet dish.

— Beans and rice usually triple in volume during cook-

One-Dish-Meal Combinations

COMBINE		ADD (FOR BINDERS)	TOP WITH
Cooked or canned,	Frozen, canned	cheese sauces	grated cheese
diced	or cooked veg.	cream sauces	pastry
seafood	peas	tomato sauce	biscuits
ham	corn	broth	crushed potato chips
pork	carrots	milk sauces	bread crumbs
beef	mushrooms	gravies	cereal flakes
(Other grains,	broccoli	white sauces	mashed potatoes
whole or cracked)	yellow squash	veg. juices	slivered olives
cheese	zucchini	soups	peppers
hard-boiled eggs	green beans	eggs	nuts
(chopped or	tomatoes		
sliced)	sprouts		
pastas	potatoes		
macaroni			
spaghetti			
noodles			

beans
(1 or more kinds)
rice
wheat
barley

hot dogs
bologna
luncheon meats
TVP products

ing. One cup uncooked makes three cups cooked. Precooked rice will not make quite as much.

—Spaghetti and macaroni usually double in volume during cooking. Two cups uncooked equals four cups cooked.

—Noodles measure almost the same uncooked as cooked. Four cups uncooked equals four to five cups cooked.

Get up early enough in the morning so you have time to prepare a casserole. It can bake while you're making a salad and setting the table. Or, one of the older children or your husband can put it in the oven before you get home. Dinner could very well be ready to put on the table shortly after you arrive.

How many times have you started to prepare a dish and then realized you didn't have all the ingredients you needed? Perhaps this list of quick substitutions will help.

80

QUICK SUBSTITUTIONS

When You Need:	Use:
1 square unsweetened chocolate	3-4 tablespoons cocoa plus 1 tablespoon shortening
1 cup whole milk	½ c evaporated milk and ½ c water or 4 tablespoons dry milk and 1 c water
1 cup sour milk	1 c sweet milk with 1 tablespoon vinegar or lemon juice added
1 tablespoon flour, for thickening	½ tablespoon cornstarch

1 teaspoon baking powder	¼ teaspoon baking soda and ¼ teaspoon cream of tartar
1 cup buttermilk	1 cup yogurt
1 whole egg	2 egg yolks or 2 tablespoons dried egg and 3 tablespoons water

81

Chapter Eight

Just for Husbands

This chapter is dedicated to my "Knight in Shining Armour." I am no "women's libber"; I enjoy being spoiled and pampered by my husband. Since I have had to work, in order for us to obtain a goal, he has done all within his capabilities to make my burden lighter. He is a fine example to our son and daughter. I truly appreciate him.

Your attitude, as the husband of a working woman, is of utmost importance in helping her cope with job, marriage, home, and children. Remember, she is working outside the home not because she wants to, but because you both decided it was necessary if you were to reach a common goal.

As one woman said: "I think patience and understanding on the part of the husband is very important. (A little help with the housework wouldn't hurt either.)"

Another said: "A workable solution is having a husband that appreciates you. As long as he is willing to share some of the burdens with you, things will turn out all right."

Husbands, throughout this book I've repeatedly advised your wives to be patient and maintain good attitudes. I know you realize that kindly attitudes and patience MUST be reciprocal qualities in a marriage.

It's the "lollipops and roses" you offer to your wife that lightens her load and keeps her the "girl" you married — a kind word; a thoughtful deed; helping it to be our house, our problem, our goal. So much pleasure and delight can be derived from an unexpected gift — be it a candy bar or a flower. These little things are the treasures that keep her your sweetheart. Only a word if she looks tired: "Honey, don't cook tonight. Let's sneak out to that fancy new restaurant in town . . . the one with the nineteen-cent hamburger." I can guarantee that that will lift the spirit of any tired working girl.

Be a hero and offer to help her with the laundry or the dishes so that you can go for a ride or a walk together later.

Talk to her. Talk to her, and then talk to her some more. Remind her of the goals, short-range and long-range, that you are struggling to obtain. Help her keep it all in perspective.

83

Be the shoulder she needs to lean on for extra strength.

Help her remember your spiritual goals as well as the temporal things you are working for.

Pray together! And pray together often.

Be understanding. Remember, your wife is working and naturally tired. A little added understanding from you will help soothe a situation or two.

Lenore Romney says it very well: "I still remember my husband saying to me, as a bride, 'If you treat a wife like a flower, she will give you perfume all of your life.' I also remember vividly an incident that resulted in one of the greatest lessons of my life. We had been married only a few weeks when I became moody one morning over some misunderstanding. When my husband returned from work, I was still in a bad mood. He became very serious as he said, 'You still can't be in a mood, because I depend on you for my happiness.' That statement hit me like a bolt.

Good grief, if he depended upon me for the greatest thing of all, happiness, he was going to get it! What a fantastically important role — to be able to bring happiness to the one you love the most."[1]

In the struggle to survive and progress in the workaday world, remember how valuable your "other half" is. As you depend on your wife for your happiness, so she depends on you for her happiness.

Remember a few encouraging words. "A little honest compliment about some particular act or trait . . . will act like the balm of Gilead."[2] We all long for encouragement.

Support your wife. Sharing her burdens will bring you closer together.

Remember to take the time to play together. If you have to "rob" the food budget to take your wife out to a movie, do so. You both need fun and companionship to ease the struggles.

All the little things count in the long run; but, for immediate results, remember those three most important words and use them often: "I love you."

[1]Lenore Romney, "Are We Liberated?" *The Joy of Being a Woman*, compiled by Duane and Jean Crowther (Horizon Publishers, Bountiful, Utah, 1972), p. 299.
[2]Harold Lundstrom, *Motherhood, A Partnership With God* (Bookcraft, Inc., Salt Lake City, Utah, 1967), p. 194.

84

Index

86

Index